Pennine Way
NORTH: Bowes to Kirk Yetholm

Tony Hopkins grew up in Derby, close to the
southern Pennines, and spent fifteen years as
an official with the Northumberland National
Park. He is now a freelance writer and
consultant in countryside interpretation. His
other books include *The Cheviot Hills: A Sense of
Wilderness* and *Northumbria: True to the Land*.

D1471993

Pennine Way

NORTH: Bowes to Kirk Yetholm

Tony Hopkins

*Photographs by Simon Warner
and Tony Hopkins*

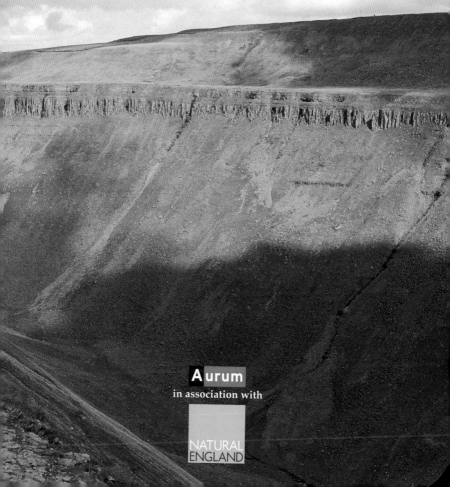

Aurum

in association with

NATURAL
ENGLAND

ACKNOWLEDGEMENTS

For their advice and information, thanks to Chris Sainty, John Weatherall, Simon Hodgson, Brian Long, Jim Givens, Dr Geoff Singleton, and Wendy Pettigrew. Special thanks also to Don and Sheila Stokoe for their company out on the hills. For past revisions, thanks to Mike Ogden, Tim Fish, Tony Jackson and Lorna McCluskey. For this and previous revisions, thanks to Steve Westwood.

This updated edition published 2010 by Aurum Press Ltd
7 Greenland Street, London NW1 0ND • www.aurumpress.co.uk
in association with Natural England.
www.naturalengland.org.uk • www.nationaltrail.co.uk

Text copyright © 1989, 1997, 2000, 2004, 2007, 2010 by Aurum Press Ltd and Natural England

Photographs on pages 57, 68, 76, 89, 103, 122, 124, 138 and 164-5 by Tony Hopkins. All other photographs copyright © 1989, 1997, 2004 by Natural England, those on pages 15, 49, 54, 72, 80, 84, 144-5, and 150 by McCoy Wynne and pages 17 and 43 by Mike Kipling, page 84 Alamy, pages 84 and 157, RSPB Images; all others by Simon Warner

A catalogue record for this book is available from the British Library.

ISBN 978 1 84513 562 1

1 3 5 7 9 10 8 6 4 2
2010 2012 2014 2013 2011

Book design by Robert Updegraff

Printed and bound in Italy by Printer Trento Srl

Cover photograph: *High Cup Nick/Alamy*
Title page photograph: *High Cup Nick* photograph by Nick Warner

Aurum Press want to ensure that these National Trail Guides are always as up to date as possible – but stiles collapse, pubs close and bus services change all the time. If, on walking this path, you discover any important changes of which future walkers need to be aware, do let us know. Either email us on **trailguides@aurumpress.co.uk** with your comments, or if you take the trouble to drop us a line to:
Trail Guides, Aurum Press, 7 Greenland Street, London NW1 0ND,
we'll send you a free guide of your choice as thanks.

CONTENTS

Circular walks appear on pages 36, 82, 95 and 140.

HOW TO USE THIS GUIDE

The 268-mile (431-kilometre) Pennine Way is covered by two National Trail guides. This book features the northern section of the Way, from Bowes to Kirk Yetholm (141 miles/225 kilometres). A companion guide features the Way from Edale in the Peak District to Bowes.

The guide is in three parts:
- The introduction, with an historical background to the trail and advice for walkers.
- The Pennine Way itself, split into nine chapters, with maps opposite the description for each route section. This part of the guide also includes information on places of interest and background features, as well as a number of circular walks which can be taken around each part of the Way. Key sites are numbered both in the text and on the maps to make it easier to follow the route description.
- The last part includes useful information, such as local transport, accommodation and organisations involved with the Way.

The maps have been prepared by the Ordnance Survey® for this Trail Guide using 1:25 000 Explorer™ or Outdoor Leisure® maps as a base. The line of the Pennine Way is shown in yellow, with the status, where known, of each section of the Way – footpath, bridleway or byway, for example – shown in green underneath (see key on inside front cover). In some cases, the yellow line on these maps may not coincide exactly with the right-of-way, or may show a route which is different from that shown in other guide books and maps; walkers are recommended to follow the yellow route in this guide, which in most cases will be the route that is waymarked with the distinctive acorn symbol 🌰 used for all National Trails. In a few places the author has given alternative routes to follow; full details are in the text. Any parts of the Way that may be difficult to follow on the ground are clearly highlighted in the route description, and important points to watch for are marked with letters in each chapter, both in the text and on the maps. *Some maps start on a right-hand page – black arrows (➡) at the edge of the maps indicate the start point.* In places, the Pennine Way is being diverted from the line shown in this guide for maintenance or repair work or to achieve a better route. Walkers are asked to follow the waymark or signs.

Distance checklist

To help you plan your accommodation along the northern part of the Pennine Way, and to check your progress, the following distances may be helpful.

location	approx. distance from previous location	
	miles	*km*
Pasture End	0	0
Baldersdale (Blackton)	3.6	5.8
[Bowes/Baldersdale] Bowes Loop	5.8	9.3
Middleton	6.0	9.7
Saur Hill/Langdon Beck	7.7	12.4
Dufton	12.3	19.8
Garrigill	15.8	25.4
Alston	3.9	6.3
Slaggyford	5.0	8.0
Greenhead	10.9	17.5
Steel Rigg/Once Brewed	6.6	10.6
Bellingham	14.5	23.3
Byrness	14.7	23.6
Chew Green	4.9	7.9
Clennell Street (for Cocklawfoot)	8.8	14.2
Kirk Yetholm (high level)	11.0	17.7
Kirk Yetholm (low level)	11.3	18.2
Kirk Yetholm (detour to The Cheviot) +	2.3	3.7

KEY MAPS

Pennine Way

4 Chapter start point

0 km   5

0 miles   5

Based on Ordnance Survey Road Map

KEY MAP 2

Preface

The Pennine Way was Britain's first long-distance footpath and was designated more than 40 years ago. This guide follows the northern section of the route, from Bowes to Kirk Yetholm in Scotland – a total distance of nearly 130 miles. It includes Cross Fell, the highest point in the Pennines, and runs alongside Hadrian's Wall for a short distance before reaching the Cheviot Hills on the Scottish border.

The peaty landscape of the Pennines has proved vulnerable to erosion by walkers and over the years a considerable investment has been made in restoration works. Undamaged peatlands are among our richest areas of biodiversity. If managed well, peatlands are a natural reservoir for carbon, which they capture and store. The nature of the terrain makes it very much a walkers' path, but Natural England is leading the development of the Pennine Bridleway, a new route that is now partly open, providing horse-riders, cyclists and walkers with a long-distance bridleway through the Pennines, specially designed for their needs.

National Trails are promoted and funded by Natural England and funded and maintained by local authorities. They are all marked with the distinctive acorn symbol, which signals that you are on the right route and serves as a sign of quality.

I hope that you will enjoy this book whilst planning your walk, and that it will enhance your pleasure on 'the backbone of England'.

Poul Christensen CBE
Chair
Natural England

PART ONE

INTRODUCTION

The origins of the Pennine Way

The Pennine Way was the first National Trail in Britain, officially opened on 24 April 1965, at a gathering of over 2,000 walkers at Malham Moor in the Yorkshire Dales. The project had gained Ministerial approval in 1951 but it took a further 14 years for local authorities to open up the 70 miles (113 km) of new paths necessary to complete the route.

The original idea for a continuous Pennine walk appeared in a *Daily Herald* article in 1935, written by the rambler and journalist Tom Stephenson. He had been impressed by similar trails in the United States and had the vision to apply the concept of a wilderness path to the English Pennines. The country was ready and the suggestion was carried forward on the same heady wind of change that had demanded access to the hills and the establishment of National Parks. Most of the fieldwork for the Pennine Way was undertaken by the Ramblers' Association and the Youth Hostels Association in the late 1930s. The war only sharpened the nation's appetite for peace and the appreciation of its heritage, so the 1949 Act was carried through Parliament in a spirit of optimism.

Sixty years later millions of people walk the countryside without considering their right to be there, which is as it should be. But there are still problems to be resolved. The Countryside Agency (now Natural England) went on to rename the original long-distance routes National Trails and establish new routes. The Pennine Way stands as the first and furthest of high-hills walks; it is a famous demonstration of how people can find peace and freedom in an over-crowded age.

Maintaining the path

Over the years the Pennine Way has become a victim of its own success. Until recently there were serious erosion problems, particularly across Peak District moorland and on popular ridge walks through the Yorkshire Dales and the Cheviots. However, a great deal of effort has now gone into repairing and improving the route; bridges and stiles have been installed, stone slabs and aggregate surfaces have replaced the worst peat-grooves. Although some traditionalists may lament the introduction of artificial surfaces, no one could ever enjoy wading through waterlogged peat.

Major repairs have brought major benefits to walkers, speeding up progress and allowing attention to stray to the landscape rather than be concentrated on placing one foot after another. Also, the repaired and resurfaced sections of the route are relatively few and far between and they settle down and weather surprisingly quickly. Some parts of the Way have been diverted on to paths better able to withstand the pressure. Things are still changing and there may be places where official waymarks and stiles clearly indicate a route that differs from the map, in which case you should always be guided by the markers on the ground.

How to walk the Way

Some people complete the Pennine Way in 10 days and complain afterwards that it was nothing more than an endurance test. (The record is held by Mike Hartley, who in 1989 ran it in 2 days, 17 hours and 20 minutes.) Others take a month and return home refreshed and happy. Personal achievement is impossible to measure against time and distance. This book sets out to guide walkers along the northern half of the Way, from Bowes in County Durham to Kirk Yetholm in the Borders. It does this in 9 sections; a companion volume deals with the southern half of the Way in 10 sections, thus implying that the whole trail should last 19 days. This is a reasonable estimate based on a sensible itinerary, but

Brown Rigg, Lunedale.

there are many alternatives. One of the pleasures of a long walk is planning it to suit yourself. Some natural units, such as the crossing of the Cheviots, make ideal weekend projects, and many day-length walks offer unrivalled opportunities to see high country. The nature of the Pennines makes it difficult to find circular routes which give a true impression of the landscape, but a few are included in this book.

Landscape along the Way

Kinder and Bleaklow apart, the landscape of the northern half of the Way from Bowes to Kirk Yetholm, as described in this book, is more rugged and remote than that of the southern half from Edale to Bowes. The grey Durham moors of Bowes and Cotherstone fall away into a series of green valleys through which flow the Balder, the Lune and the Tees Rivers. After the meadows and pastures of Upper Teesdale the Way gains height until the broad cleft of High Cup, the most impressive landscape feature on the entire route, leads west into the Eden Valley. From the village of Dufton the Way begins to climb again, higher and higher until it is following the East Pennine ridge culminating in Cross Fell. A 'corpse road' then descends into the South Tyne Valley and the little town of Alston, which reflects the ebb and flow of North Pennine industries and now lies at the heart of the most extensive Area of Outstanding Natural Beauty in Britain.

North of Alston the Way flanks the South Tyne again before crossing desolate Blenkinsopp Common and arriving at Greenhead on the Tyne–Solway Gap. The Way enters Northumberland National Park here, heading east along the Whin Sill and sharing the route of the Hadrian's Wall National Trail for several miles before turning north again to cross the forests and fields of Wark and so arrive at the market town of Bellingham. The open moors and wastes of Redesdale, a wilderness created out of centuries of Border conflict, carry the Way north again, only to plunge into the dark forest of Kielder. Near the head of Redesdale, Byrness marks the last settlement on the route before the curtain of forest is drawn back to reveal the Cheviot massif and the dramatic Border Ridge. Kirk Yetholm, on the banks of Bowmont Water and a few miles south-east of Kelso and the River Tweed, lies at the end of the journey.

It took millions of years to create the bedrock of the British landscape, but the effects of climate and the introduction of farming have changed the complexion of even the remotest hills

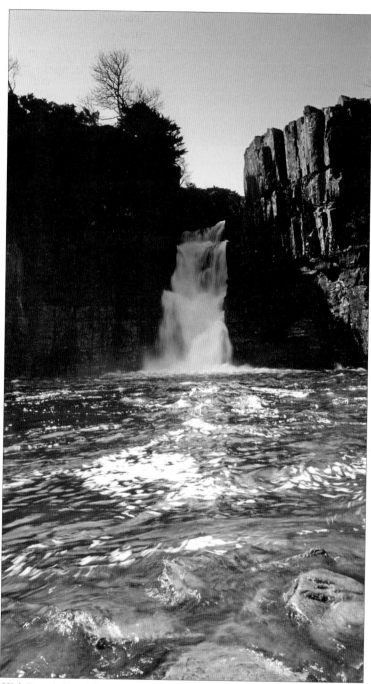

High Force in Teesdale, one of the most impressive waterfalls to be found in Britain.

High Cup, a cleft in the Pennine ridge west of the Cumbrian/Durham border.

in a fraction of that time. Seven thousand years ago most of the Pennines would have been covered in trees or scrub, but an increase in rainfall and the clearance of the primary woodland caused a build-up of peat and the beginning of mires and bogs.

The British climate has changed several times since then, but it is now in a cool and wet phase – especially in the uplands – and blanket bog pervades the Pennines as it has for centuries. The terrain of the route is variable. There are paths along river gravels and through meadows, and along dry grassy ridges with scree and rocky scrambles, but there are also long and dreary stretches of black, waterlogged peat.

Planning your walk

The Pennine Way can be a dangerous place, so preparation is important. Anyone who has never tried hill walking should test themselves over a few days or weekends in the Lake District or the Brecon Beacons before deciding to take on the Pennine Way. Many young people find they are naturally fit but lack stamina. People over 40 still have the potential for excellent stamina but lack fitness. It is never too late to get fit, but the older you are the more gentle should be the programme. Some kind of aerobic or heart and lung exercise (which gets you sweaty and breathless) for 20 minutes every two or three days is an ideal level of preparation, and can be built up gradually. If you can cope with this sort of routine, through such activities as swimming or jogging, then a day or two on the Pennine Way should hold no fears at all. However, to cope with the whole walk, day after day, requires extra stamina which can only be earned the hard way, on the hills.

The likeliest reasons for having to drop out of a long walk are blisters or sore feet. Boots should be thoroughly worn in and socks should be absorbent and without lumpy seams. Hardening the skin on the soles and heels, by applying alcohol (surgical spirit) for a few weeks before a big walk, helps to prevent blisters from forming. If they do form, prick them and apply a porous plaster which will keep the dead skin in place over the tender new layer underneath. Bruised toenails can be avoided by keeping them clipped and making sure boots fit properly in the first place.

A walker's first-aid kit should contain a few plasters, paracetamol and codeine tablets, something to treat diarrhoea, something to treat midge bites (hydrocortisone cream rather than antihistamine, which can cause a reaction) and insect repellent (e.g. oil of citronella). Lipsalve can help wind-dried lips and Vaseline can soothe sore or chapped skin in unexpected parts of the body. It is a great help to know a little about first aid, and to be aware of the treatment for gastroenteritis (drink clear fluids with glucose and a little salt), exposure (glucose, warm dry clothing and a quick walk down to shelter) and adder bites (seldom fatal but should not be ignored – immobilise the affected area and seek medical advice). Most people who get into trouble on exposed sections of the Pennine Way are ill-equipped and ill-prepared.

Essential clothing for a day on the Pennines should include a set of waterproofs (cagoule and overtrousers), a pair of warm trousers and a pullover. You may not need all of these items (shorts and T-shirt may suffice on certain memorable days) but they should be packed in the rucksack just in case. Heavyweight mountain boots can be uncomfortable and may take months or years to wear in. You may prefer modern lightweight leather walking boots, with ankle support (to reduce the risk of sprained ankles) and a degree of waterproofing. They are very much better than trainers even on dry ground. Fully enclosed gaiters (such as the Yeti type) and strong mountain boots will keep your feet dry even after crossing Kinder or The Cheviot. A good rucksack deserves as much loyalty as a comfortable pair of boots. Some are top-heavy, some have narrow or slipping straps and some absorb rainwater like a sponge. Some do all these things and still cost a lot of money. Side-pockets are useful, allowing you to separate small items you may need in a hurry. Into the main rucksack should go a compass and a set of appropriate maps, so don't forget this book!

Food and an adequate supply of drink (probably more than you think) and money (ditto) complete the basic list, to which can be added camera, notebook and whatever else you feel inclined to take with you. Company, or the deliberate avoidance of it, will of course be the nub of one of the most important decisions before the start of the walk. Safety, making sure someone knows where you are, is even more important for lone walkers than it is for groups.

Anyone undertaking the whole walk will also need to think carefully about accommodation, whether they are youth hostelling, bed and breakfasting or camping, for this will affect how much they carry and where they need to pick up provisions. Useful information, including a list of addresses to write to, appears on page 160.

PART TWO

PENNINE WAY NORTH
Bowes to Kirk Yetholm

1 Bowes to Forest-in-Teesdale

past Middleton-in-Teesdale and High Force
19 miles (30.6 km)

If you are walking direct from Keld via Tan Hill to Baldersdale, having followed the first volume of this guide, by now you will be at the A66 above God's Bridge and should continue northwards following the route described below. If you are starting from Bowes or have followed the 'Bowes loop' and are continuing on to Forest-in-Teesdale turn to pages 27 and 28.

ROUTE 1: FROM THE PENNINE WAY SOUTH

Cross the A66 via the underpass to the left. On the far side of the road, and to the left of the house and barn of Pasture End, the route heads uphill beside a wall, then bears north-east towards the bracken-covered slope of Ravock, before turning back north-west to make for a cairn and the ruins of a stone hut called Ravock Castle. The path is not always clear but once over the crest of the hill a straight wall on the far side of Deep Dale marks the route. There is a concrete footbridge over the whisky-coloured waters of Deepdale Beck.

Bowes Moor is at its best in August and September when the heather is in flower; May and June are enlivened by golden plovers and curlews, and some impressive insects including the emperor, fox and northern eggar moths.

At God's Bridge the River Greta disappears beneath the limestone.

24

Contours are given in metres
The vertical interval is 10m

25

Once across Deep Dale the Way goes through a gate and follows a path beside a drystone wall, climbing via several false crests to Race Yate Rigg. On this broad ridge the wall is left behind and Bowes Moor merges into Cotherstone Moor. In rain or mist this sweep of featureless waste is daunting and it is wise to use a compass, but in good visibility Baldersdale and its reservoirs are in sight and the route descends along a straight path across grassy or mossy moorland, keeping well left of Burners Hill to meet a road just south of Clove Lodge Farm **F**.

At this point the alternative routes merges and this section is continued on page 31 (route description) and page 30 (map). If, however, you are starting out from Bowes itself, the next section describes the route from Bowes to Baldersdale.

Contours are given in metres
The vertical interval is 10m

Bowes Castle, the ultimate defensive system of its day, was already a useless ruin 500 years ago.

ROUTE 2: BOWES TO BALDERSDALE

Bowes has known busier days. The village occupies a strategic position on the Stainmore Gap; the Romans built a fort here to defend the road linking Watling Street at Penrith with Dere Street (the northern extension of Ermine Street) at Scotch Corner. The levelled site of the fort, called Lavatrae, was used again in the 12th century when a Norman keep was built on the spot **1**. Unfortunately this was squabbled over by everyone from kings and archbishops to terrorists and outlaws, and by the mid 14th century it was little more than a ruin – but such a substantial ruin that the very thick walls are still standing today.

At the end of the main street, opposite West End Farm, there is an unusual square house **2**, now a private dwelling but once a sort of transport café and originally a school managed by a gentlemen called William Shaw. In January 1838 Charles Dickens came to stay at the nearby Unicorn Inn and was so impressed by William Shaw's Academy that he caricatured it as Dotheboys Hall in *Nicholas Nickleby*. Whether the place was quite so horrific as the one he portrayed is debatable but it is quite possible in the hard times of early Victorian England. William Shaw, the original Wackford Squeers, and George Ashton Taylor, who is supposed to have inspired the character Smike, are buried in the churchyard close by.

Under a slight cloud of Dickensian depression, the Way follows a tarmac road across the busy bypass of the A66 trunk road and heads north-west uphill with rushy moorland on either side. Notices appear warning of the dangers of poisonous gas. Old Air Ministry buildings and storage sheds have been demolished but their foundations and floors remain, and the signs speed you on your way in a state of unutterable gloom. For once the abundance of redshanks, snipe, lapwings and curlews only compounds the feeling that you are in an unwholesome, unpeopled wilderness. Rather than bear left to Tute Hill along the official route it is possible to keep north along the road, past Stoney Keld and Strand Foot, then west, staying with the road until it reaches West Stoney Keld, at which the Way bears right (north-west) along a track and through a gate and into open pasture. Past a ruined barn a path bears west-north-west above Levy Pool, then drops down to pass close by the farm. These moors have a high number of derelict steadings; hard work and poverty, and the lure of new industries, broke up the rural communities.

Levy Pool **3** has a fascinating roof, partly heather-thatched and partly stone-slabbed. A track leads through a gate below the outbuildings. The Way crosses the bridge over the Deepdale Beck and heads north. At **A** it crosses featureless rough terrain over grassy ridges towards the marshy Hazelgill Beck. Between here and **B** used to be a navigational nightmare for walkers, with very few reliable landmarks on the ground by which to plot one's course. However, the route here has now been marked out by a line of white posts: just follow them and you won't go astray. The whole area to the east of the wall is Ministry of Defence land, with warning notices and red flags.

Once through the gate **C** (*see map on page 31, continuing below*) there are excellent views across a wide sweep of moorland. The Way takes a clear line, heading north-west and making for a point just to the right of the significant gritstone outcrop of Goldsborough **D**. This part of Cotherstone Moor has more character than Sled Dale but the route is still indistinct. A compass is essential. The moor is inhabited by Swaledale sheep but fewer moorland birds, and the vegetation is poor. Several rocks along the route bear cup and ring marks, complex patterns carved during the Bronze Age. Away to the right (north-east) the drainage runs to a gap at the headwater of Yawd Sike with views beyond of the Hamsterley Fells.

The Way continues west-north-west, below the hard face of Goldsborough, then angles northwards over the crest of the ridge to pick up a path north-west, down to Baldersdale and an unfenced road. At this road the official route turns left, then right along a drive **E** to East Friar Farm before heading westward to the end of Blackton Reservoir. This route is seldom used and it is a better idea to stay with the road which heads west-north-west below Burners Hills with the flat-topped and cairned hill of Shacklesborough in the far distance.

Just beyond Hagworm Hall the well-trodden path of the direct Pennine Way route from Keld leads out on to the road from the left **F**.

Contours are given in metres
The vertical interval is 10m

The Way arcs north along the road, and down to Clove Lodge. Through the gate it crosses the yard and bears left, then heads downhill to cross a little bridge with a meandering stream and the reservoir to the right; here all the possible routes are united. The Way heads north over the larger Blackton Bridge **G** with the grassed dam wall of Baldershead Reservoir to the left. The Baldersdale reservoirs, and those yet to be encountered in the Lune Valley to the north, gather the ample rainfall of Stainmore and were created to control the Tees and to slake the industrial thirst of Cleveland.

From Blackton Bridge the Way climbs eastwards, above the shallow head of the reservoir, through Birk Hat where a path leads left (north) down to a step-stile through a wall, then uphill through pastures and meadows. One of the meadows, called 'Hannah's Meadow', is a wildlife reserve. A converted barn provides information about the work of the Trust. The 'Hannah' referred to in the name is Hannah Hauxwell, a solitary Daleswoman who found unlikely celebrity in the 1970s through a TV documentary about her arduous life on this isolated farm. She went on to ride the Orient Express and meet the Pope. Past High Birk Hat the Way continues up to a road, turning left then right and uphill again over rushy pasture. On the brow of the hill **4** there are views ahead over Lunedale and Teesdale (which lies to the north-east), and to the left over Hunderthwaite Moor.

Contours are given in metres
The vertical interval is 10m

The Way now drops down into the Lune Valley, following a wall at first, then moving away from this to cross a stile at a gate in the bottom wall and making for the farm buildings of Beck Head. Below lie two reservoirs, the impressive dam wall and spillway of Selset to the left **5** and Grassholme to the right. Grassholme's marshy shallows, between Selset Weir and the side road to Grassholme Farm, are designated a nature reserve **6** and during the spring and summer a large colony of black-headed gulls make it a noisy and bustling place. There is a path diagonally across meadows towards the road at How. A sign asks walkers to keep in single file. This makes obvious sense in June when the hay crop is knee-high and flecked with flowers, but for much of the year the meadows are indistinguishable from pastures and are grazed by sheep or cattle.

At the road the Way bears right then sharp left around the converted farmstead. Walk down to cross the reservoir at a bridge **H**, then climb the road to Grassholme Farm **I**. This is another diversion for the sake of the hay crop, through the farmyard and north along a clear path. The Way then leads uphill through a patchwork of meadows, from barn to barn and eventually to a road. Directly across the road, a track leads to Wythes Hill Farm, at which the Way bears left and goes down a walled track, then across a stream and through a gate, and finally north-east and east over rough pasture towards a field barn **J**. The route is now indistinct but the going is easy.

From the barn the Way contours around Harter Fell. The views have changed; away to the south and south-west are the high fells of Yorkshire and Cumbria, but the middle distance is now dominated by a network of meadows and fertile pastures crowding Teesdale and Lunedale. Cutting the corner of the ridge, with the old workings of Greengates Quarry to the right **7**, the Way stays on the middle contour of the hill and passes through several old walled pastures before dropping down along a well-marked grassy path, heading north-east towards the town of Middleton-in-Teesdale.

The knoll at the end of the ridge to the right (east) is Kirkcarrion **8**, a Bronze Age tumulus or burial site now planted with pines. It is visible for miles around, but is the sort of place that no footpath ever goes near. For centuries people have avoided it and children are afraid of seeing ghosts there. Over the past few years archeologists have accepted the spiritual significance of such places. If they scare us now, they probably scared our ancestors; or acted as the cultural centrepiece of a community.

Contours are given in metres
The vertical interval is 10m

33

The cairned path heads down over rolling pasture to a gate in the field corner **K**, then continues more steeply to cross an old railway line, long dismantled, and emerge on a side road (*see map on page 35, continuing below*). The Way turns right then left along the main road, the B6277 north towards Middleton, but before the Tees bridge **L** it turns left along a track and leads through meadowland on the south bank of the Tees. For a while the path stays away from the river bank. To the north is Middleton **9**, a Saxon settlement which expanded dramatically in the 18th century when the 'Quaker Company' – the London Lead Company – opened mines in the area. To the south beyond the river terrace lies the Whin Sill, a cliff of quartz-dolerite, similar to basalt. This narrow ribbon of rock extends across northern England and forms some

Contours are given in metres
The vertical interval is 10m

of the most impressive scenery of the Pennine Way. In many places the Whin Sill has been quarried for roadstone, and Crossthwaite **10** is the first of many cavities in the face of the Sill.

Where Rowton Beck meets the Tees **M**, east of Holwick, the Way at last drops down to the river bank and in summer the day becomes a gentle liaison with the river. Dippers, grey wagtails, common sandpipers and goosanders fly up and down, and the alder and sallow bushes are full of willow warblers, blackcaps and redstarts. Heavy rainfall, particularly in winter and spring, can make the liaison a deafening one-way tirade; the Tees is not as tame as it looks and it is best to treat it with respect.

Past Scoberry Bridge, and on to Wynch Bridge **11**, a little suspension bridge down from Bowlees on the B6277, the Way softens into a local beauty spot. The original Wynch Bridge was built in 1704 and was used by miners, but in 1820 it collapsed, killing one man. The present bridge was built in 1830. Here the Way enters the Teesdale National Nature R

Contours are given in metres
The vertical interval is 10m

35

Rivers erode their beds until they reach harder rock, at which point they form steps or nick points. Whinstone is extremely hard and several famous waterfalls are to be found where the Sill outcrops. The first and least dramatic of these is Low Force **12**, a pretty place, ideal for a picnic, but uncomfortably popular. It is here that walkers begin to notice unusual flowers, the special plants that have given Teesdale its international reputation (see page 53). Globe flower is abundant, and the rocks have patches of both shrubby and alpine cinquefoil. Further on, just past Holwick Head Bridge, the Way climbs along a well-used path to a stile **N**. The number of people walking this route was threatening to damage the wildlife habitat – hence the artificial path. The first thing you notice about the path above Keedholm Scar **13** is that the bushes clothing the slopes grow either tall and thin or low and wide, but they are all junipers. Juniper wood, known as savin, was once used to make the best charcoal for use in the gunpowder industry, and the berries were harvested to flavour London gin. In the middle of the dream-like experience of the ancient junipers you begin to hear a distant sound of thunder and soon a view of High Force **14** is gained by following a short path to the right. This is by far the best way to see this most famous of falls. On the far bank you have to pay and elbow your way past shoals of tourists; here you can pretend to be alone. High Force crashes from a shelf of dolerite over a horizontal band of shale to a deep dark plunge pool 69 feet (21 metres) below. The water is always brown and peaty, and very cold. Considering its stature, High Force is remarkably unspoilt; less so than many of the 'awesome' little Lakeland cataracts.

CIRCULAR WALK: UPPER TEESDALE AND CRONKLEY FELL

11½ miles (18.5 km) **(see maps on pages 37–39)**

This walk is a good introduction to Teesdale. Park in the lay-by on the B6277 at Bowlees between High Force and Middleton-in-Teesdale and walk down to the river at Wynch Bridge **11**, then follow the path uphill to contour westwards on the lower fell slopes. This leads quite steeply on to Cronkley Fell, then down to the River Tees which is then followed back to the Wynch Bridge.

Contours are given in metres
The vertical interval is 10m

The Pennine Way leads out of the woodland beside the top of High Force, then heads upstream (*see map on page 39*). The Tees subsides into a ribbon of blue water again; the thunder dies and is replaced by the call of sandpipers, oystercatchers and redshanks. On the north bank a sizeable slice of the hillside has been taken away by a quarry **15**. Beside this is Dine Holm Scar, which has tiers of heather and juniper. Bracken Rigg **16** is free of bracken but also has an ageing crop of junipers. The official route contours to the left (south) side, via two stiles over fenced enclosures. Incidentally, on the crest of the hill, where the scatter of trees opens out, there are good views of the fells to the south of Cronkley and the cairned summit of Noon Hill. The ridge of Bracken Rigg leads westwards and the Pennine Way takes this easy line down towards a fence but bears right

Contours are given in me
The vertical interval is 1

to a stile. The way continues beside a wall to another stile, then down a gully and so to Cronkley Farm. From here a track heads north to a prominent bridge, used by farm vehicles. It is now possible either to take a footpath **O** north-east to Forest-in-Teesdale or to head along the Way on the north bank of the Tees, past the confluence of Harwood Beck, and turn right at the next footbridge up to the B6277 and the hamlet of Langdon Beck, where there is a youth hostel.

A long day, and not the most exhilarating of walks, but if it is early summer there will be ample recompense in the beauty of the flower-studded meadows and riverside pastures.

25 km or 15½ miles

Above Wynch Bridge the Tees is at its most picturesque.

Swaledale sheep grazing the fells of Upper Teesdale. Winter can be a testing time.

Levy Pool

Crumbling barns and cottages are a common sight on the Pennines. For many years the ruin of Levy Pool **3**, near Bowes, attracted special attention from Pennine Way walkers because in younger days it had so clearly been a thriving and lively place. Children had been born and raised here, had grown up to farm and raised farming families. Eventually times changed and the sons of Levy Pool sought their livelihoods elsewhere. Recently a new owner has renovated the place, rebuilt the crumbling gables and chimney of the farmhouse and had the roof rethatched. Thus, what had seemed a few years ago to be a sad ruin is now a fascinating insight into the past.

The steading of Levy Pool faces south, its back to the steep bank above Deepdale Beck. The main row of buildings comprises barn, farmhouse, cow-shed ('byre'), stalls, outhouse and cart shed. The farmhouse has perfectly square windows with solid sandstone sills and lintels, and the lintel above the inner door bears the date mark 1776. Originally all the roofs were thatched with heather, following a tradition dating back at least to medieval times, requiring a high gable with a steeply pitched roof to repel rain and snow. On some of the buildings sandstone flags or slates had replaced the 'black-thack' long before the steading reached the end of its working life. The roofs were composed of bolted A-frames and sawn cross-beams. Rows of closely spaced rafters, mostly untrimmed trunks of young pine trees. were nailed to the ridge and supported on headstones at the eaves. A foot-thick blanket of heather completed the job. The recent rebuild has followed the traditional methods as far as possible, and the result is an attractive and authentic renovation.

Only a handful of heather-thatched farmhouses and cottages survive in England. All the natural building materials were readily available here at Levy Pool before the First World War, but there are now few living pines or heather bushes within sight of the farm. In fact, the remnants of the plantation on the hillside behind the farm have only recently been cleared. The dead pines were found to be full of shrapnel, the legacy of army training exercises. However, young trees have now been planted on the hill and around the building, so in 50 years Levy Pool will closely resemble the 1916 version.

2 Forest-in-Teesdale to Dufton

via Cauldron Snout and High Cup
13¹/₄ miles (21.3 km)

Saur Hill Bridge **A** is a good place from which to contemplate a day's walk, though this part of the Pennine Way has no obvious point of start (or finish if walking south) so the choice is arbitrary. The bridge spans Harwood Beck, wide and shallow and ever-changing. Redshanks and oystercatchers call from the nearby pastures; grey and yellow wagtails hawk for flies along banks and dippers usually nest in the stonework below. Old signs here may inform you that it is 121 miles (195 km) to Kirk Yetholm and 149 miles (240 km) to Edale; these measurements follow Wainwright and add up to 270 miles (435 km), which is his total estimate for the walking distance of the Pennine Way.

From the bridge the Way follows a track to Saur Hill Farm ('Sayer Hill' on the map) but angles up to the left in front of the farm and continues along an ill-defined path across meadowland and over a step-stile, and so across pastures and past a national nature reserve sign, making for the gap to the north (right) of Cronkley Fell. The River Tees is heard before it is seen, a conversational jumble of sounds accompanied in summer by piping sandpipers, which nest on the gravels, and redshank, which nest among the marsh grasses.

The Way stays beside the river and carries on to a track **B**, by-passing Widdy Bank Farm **17**. The little farm, like most of its neighbours on the north side of the river, was part of the Raby estate, reputed to stretch most of the way to Darlington. The original shell of the farmhouse dates back to 1698; hundreds of coats of whitewash help to keep the walls wind- and weatherproof. The application of whitewash is part of the lease agreement – hence all the white farm buildings in Teesdale. The farm (now a base for Natural England staff managing the NNR) extends to 2,000 acres (809 hectares), mostly of very rough grazing with just 30 acres (12 hectares) of hay, so most winter feed has to be brought in as silage. A few cattle graze in the fields by the farms but the wild fells are the territory of hardy Swalesdale sheep.

Part of the route keeps to the track, close beside the Tees. For centuries the river marked the boundary between the North Riding of Yorkshire and County Durham. Now the county line lies further south but the two sides of the dale are in separate ownership (the land south of the river is part of the Earl of Strathmore's estate) and so have different traditions, reflected in every farmhouse and field.

The Tees snakes its way between high fells composed of sedimentary rock (the typical cycle of limestone-shale-sandstone) but influenced by fire. Silurian slate, 500 million years old, underlies the Carboniferous sediments; soft green slate was once quarried nearby and made into pencils. (The 'widdy' was a local name for the slate pencils.) However, the most important geological event occurred less than 300 million years ago, when violent earthquakes forced molten rock between existing sediments. The rock itself cooled to form quartz-dolerite, exposed in Teesdale as the Whin Sill. Minerals were deposited in the faults, creating a stockpile of metal ores, and limestone was hardened and fractured into granules which outcropped as beds of 'sugar limestone' and were later colonised by arctic-alpine flowers (see page 53). Thus, whether visitors come to Teesdale for the views, the industrial history or the wildlife, the key lies in a single fiery episode at the end of the Carboniferous period.

Contours are given in metres
The vertical interval is 10m

The path is easy to follow but it is difficult underfoot in places. Scree and boulder-fields alternate with boardwalks and flagstones, making walking hazardous. Any spare attention should go to the steep rocky slopes and cliffs (or 'clints') to the right **18**, but if you can make a few stops along the way they may pay dividends.

This is a good place to look for ring ouzels, which are unusually common here. They may be closely related to blackbirds but are very shy and inclined to fly away rather than sit and display their white crescent-mark. An elusive soot-coloured thrush among the rowan bushes and whinstone boulders may well turn out to be a ring ouzel – especially if it goes 'peeoo' rather than 'pink pink'. However, when scared or close to its nest the ouzel goes 'teckteck', just like a blackbird.

Falcon Clints **19** are impressive, the hard whinstone geometry mellowed by green dabs of ferns and map lichen. Kestrels are often in evidence; other falcons (such as peregrines and merlins) are possible, but they are likely to be less obvious than the kestrel with its distinctive hovering flight.

The Pennine Way stays close to the foot of the clints, turning north with the Tees opposite the confluence of the Maize Beck **C**. The path leads beside grassy river verges or scrambles its way over tumbled columns of dolerite, like the fallen ruins of a Greek temple. Years of wear by the feet of tourists have polished the boulders along the path and made them a hazard in wet weather. Twisted ankles and broken hips are regular mishaps on this section.

The noise of angry water has by now ushered in another waterfall. From this approach Cauldron Snout **20** is an explosive torrent, a broad fan of white spray escaping from a narrow cleft in the Whin Sill. The stone buttresses on the shoulders of the waterfall are a convenient place to stop for a lunch break. Take the opportunity to enjoy the vision of an untamed Tees **D**; at the top of the rock climb lies the dam wall of Cow Green Reservoir **21**. The reservoir was the subject of a public inquiry in the 1960s.

The Tees is crossed, and Cumbria is entered, by meeting a metalled track and following this westward. The Way stays with the track as it heads south-west to Birkdale. There are good views back along the upper Tees and over Cronkley Fell, and south to Mickle Fell, which rises to 2,585 feet (788 metres). Birkdale **E**, which is a mountain rescue sub-post, is approached by keeping to the track and going through the farmyard (*see map on page*

Contours are given in metres
The vertical interval is 10m

continuing below). Once across the Grain Beck **F** the whole atmosphere of the walk changes. East is giving way to west; even the sheep are from Dufton, where the farms have fell-grazing rights as far as Cow Green.

A new 'Hymac' or artificial path now leads safely over the boggy ground to a cairn by the old mine spoil of Moss Shop **22**. 'Shop' was the name given to very basic bunkhouse accommodation provided for miners on the fells; at weekends they returned to their homes. Mickle Fell lies across the Maize Beck to the left (south-east), Meldon Hill rises 2,487 feet (758 metres) to the right (north-north-west).

From Moss Shop the route leads along a 'Hymac' path through a sike (a steep-sided narrow stream). At the head of the sike the route follows a stone-flagged path alongside a ditch before becoming indistinct as it leads ahead past posts and cairns. The most reliable guides are the small clapper bridges over the side-streams. Eventually, the route heads down to meet the Maize Beck **G.** The landscape is bleak and treeless – there are no dwellings in sight, and no sounds to be heard except for the calls of larks and pipits, curlews and golden plovers.

After travelling through such a lonely land the Maize Beck is a welcome relief. The walk along its bank, beside shelves of limestone colonised by pearlwort and thyme, is idyllic but brief. Maize Beck is crossed by a footbridge beyond a waymarked sign **H**.

Contours are given in metres
The vertical interval is 10m

Cauldron Snout waterfall.

Contours are given in metres
The vertical interval is 10m

49

The path now follows the old miners' route to High Cup Nick **I**, the most impressive feature on the northern section of the Pennine Way. Try to avoid taking short cuts across the soft peat; this is a sensitive landscape and offers the nearest thing to a wilderness that you will experience.

After crossing the beck and heading west-south-west up the clear path to High Cup Plain **J** it is possible to approach the head of the valley at the nick of High Cup Gill and so find yourself at the pivotal point of the whole landscape **K** (*see map on page 51, continuing below*). The world suddenly opens out beneath you. A curtain of sheer whinstone cliffs sweeps left and right, beneath which cascades of grass and scree curve inwards to create a deep basin. The effect is stunning; although on a lesser scale, the sensation is akin to standing on the edge of the Rift Valley. Ravens and peregrines patrol the grey columns of dolerite. At the foot of the amphitheatre, High Cup

Contours are given in metres
The vertical interval is 10m

Gill **23**, like a fine silver thread stitched into rugged tweed, traces its way south-west to the Eden Valley. Beyond lie the Lakeland fells.

A path bears right, at first close to the edge of the precipice but soon along a safe grassy bank, heading south-west above a stack of rock called Nichol Chair **L**. In good visibility the far wall of High Cup seems close enough to touch, but it is getting further away by the minute as the widening valley opens out to Middletongue Crag. The Pennines melt away; all that remains is the descent into the Vale of Eden.

Cairns mark the rocky downhill path. But Dufton provides the only possible overnight stop. There is no path across the treacherous fells to cut the corner, and in any case it is a long way to Garrigill.

Contours are given in metres
The vertical interval is 10m

The path drops down to an old drove road **M** which leads directly to the village of Dufton **24**. Green rolling pastures, cobwebbed by drystone walls, appear on either side of the track, and hedgerows of blackthorn and gooseberry soften the roadside as it reaches Town Head **N**. Here, the Way turns right along the main road towards the village before turning north close to the Methodist church. Dufton is a picturesque interlude. It is possible for the walker to rest by sitting on the village green **O** outside the pub or youth hostel and see where you have come from or where you will be going to. The Way could not be better served.

3 km or 2 miles
Appleby-in-Westmoorland

Contours are given in metres
The vertical interval is 10m

The Teesdale rarities

Anyone with a knowledge of wild flowers will have heard of Upper Teesdale, particularly since the late 1960s when a public inquiry was held to consider the case against flooding part of the famous Widdybank Fell to form Cow Green Reservoir. Eventually Parliament approved the reservoir scheme and the valley was flooded in 1971–72 but the flowers still remain on the adjacent fells, a little rarer, a little more restricted in their range.

For many years no one could explain why such places as Teesdale and Ben Lawers in Scotland seemed to have more than their share of special flowers, but in 1949 Sir Harry Godwin suggested they were fragments of a carpet of tundra vegetation which had covered most of Britain after the Ice Age but had then been shaded out by trees when the climate improved. One of Teesdale's great rarities, the dwarf birch, occurs in one small patch and radiocarbon dating of leaf and pollen remains in the peat underneath it has provided a continuous inch-by-inch record stretching back 10,000 years. Thus it appears that Teesdale was a grassy island in a sea of forest, and its plants have been able to cope with the belated arrival of farming and any subsequent changes in the climate.

The living history of the landscape is impressive, but in practice much of Teesdale looks unremarkable and its commonest plants are those found everywhere. Daisies and dandelions, and a host of other weeds, probably arrived as seeds on animals' hoofs or walkers' boots. The dominant communities of the unimproved pasture include tormentil and heath bedstraw, as they do on most other stretches of the Pennine Way. However, the close combination of primary habitats, marsh and bog, riverside, scree, upland heath and limestone grassland make this one of the best places to stop for a few minutes to see the flowers of the uplands.

The most unusual habitat is the 'sugar limestone' found on Widdybank and Cronkley Fells. When the Whin Sill was created, from molten rock pushed up through the earth's crust nearly 300 million years ago, the strata next to the hot rock was metamorphosed, and in the case of the existing limestone a crumbly sort of marble was the result. The Pennine Way does not lead across the plateaux on which most of this sugar limestone is found, but there are outcrops or shelves on several of the slopes and it is possible to find most of the lime-loving plants by following the becks radiating away from the main valley.

It is usually possible to criss-cross the Maize Beck, but after a storm the stream may be

...angerous torrent.

The most famous Teesdale plant is the spring gentian, a low-growing and short-lived perennial which produces a large, five-petalled flower, a vivid and unforgettable blue in colour. The flowers open only on bright sunny days and the season is short and variable. Sometimes the plant is in seed by the end of May, sometimes it is still out at the end of June. Sometimes the flowers are prolific, at other times they are sparse. Unpredictability added to rarity (Western Ireland is the only other British locality) make the spring gentian an aristocrat.

By contrast, the Teesdale violet is a rather untidy little plant despite its rarity. It grows on broken limey ground, especially where there are lots of molehills, and is smaller and more pink than other violets. Often Teesdale violets grow alongside bird's-eye primrose and suffer by comparison; the pastel shades and

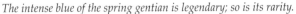

The intense blue of the spring gentian is legendary; so is its rarity.

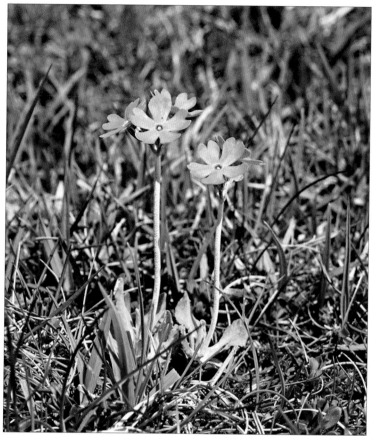

Bird's-eye primrose is a speciality of the North Yorks Pennines.

neat structure of the pink-flowered primrose make it one of the prettiest of plants, less gaudy than the gentian, more finely formed than the violet. These three plants probably symbolise Teesdale's flora to most people.

At the right time of year a walk through Teesdale on the Pennine Way should produce shrubby cinquefoil, globeflower, wood cranesbill, yellow and meadow saxifrage and a host of other local plants. The real rarities, such as alpine forget-me-not, mountain avens, bitter milkwort, alpine bartsia and bog sandwort, are not so easy to find and often occur in restricted localities on the fell tops. Teesdale is a national nature reserve and ramdom trampling is frowned on. It would be a tragedy if a plant had managed to survive for more than 10,000 years only to be exterminated by a misplaced boot.

3 Dufton to Alston

via Great Dun Fell and Garrigill
19³/₄ miles (31.8 km)

In poor weather the North Pennines can test the heart of any walker, and avoiding poor weather requires luck rather than judgement. The headwaters of the Tees lattice a windswept plateau of moorland, rising in the west to a chain of mighty hills. This section of the Way begins in the verdant valley of the River Eden, then climbs sharply to Knock Fell and heads north-west to link the summits of Dun Fell and Cross Fell, before arcing north-east over open moors and commons to reach the South Tyne at Garrigill, and thence along the river to Alston. A long day, strenuous at first but earning the reward of incomparable views. Few other sections of the trail cast so potent a spell.

Dufton was a lead-mining village, yet it lacks the hard edge of Alston or Middleton and is built around a tree-lined green. Garden gates are overhung by rose and honeysuckle and the walls are part-hidden by clumps of toadflax and corydalis. At first sight, Dufton has an enviable air of prosperity and seems more West Country than Westmorland. The Pennine Way leaves the main road close to the Methodist church **A**, beside Dufton Hall and a converted cottage bearing the inscription LWONIN FYEAT 1648. The words may look Welsh but are actually local dialect for Lane (or Lonnen) Foot. The route heads north-east along a track, then north-west along a path called Hurning Lane (used by miners when the fells were full of small lead mines). This route has been reinstated after years of neglect, when it had virtually turned into a stretch of marshland.

The back lanes of Dufton present a very different face of the village, battened down against the Helm Wind. This fierce and infamous blast is caused when an easterly airflow rushes downhill to meet the warm air mass of the Eden Valley; the 'helm' refers to an associated helmet or pall of cloud hanging over Cross Fell.

At the western end of the village the alternative route turns right along the road and heads downhill, then bears right along a track signed 'Pennine Way via Great Dun Fell'. This leads back on to the official route along a hawthorn-lined track, past Coatsike Farm **B**. The track resolves itself into Hurning Lane, lined with thorn and ash trees. Ash was widely planted in previous centuries because it was so useful – it was palatable to

Dufton Hall Farm in Cumbria.

Contours are given in metres
The vertical interval is 10m

59

The old clapper bridge over Great Rundale Beck.

hungry stock and the wood could be worked into tool handles or used as a domestic fuel.

Before the recent management work it used to be much easier to walk beside this forgotten byway than along it; no string of pack ponies has followed this road for generations and it used to be overhung with clutching branches. There is still an air of haunted neglect about the place. Halsteads **C**, the next farm along, is deserted and has a similar bitter-sweet atmosphere. Beyond this the Way contours around Cosca Hill, from where there is a wonderful view back across the Eden Valley to the Lakeland fells.

Great Rundale Beck is crossed at an old clapper bridge **25**, the stone slabs worn smooth by the comings and goings of shepherds, miners and long-distance walkers.

The whole character of the terrain now begins to change on the gradual ascent north-east towards the high fells. The gentle lowlands are left behind and rough pasture and moorland appear. Curlews call, snipe drum and buzzards soar overhead. Away to the left (north-west) is Knock Pike **26** which, like Dufton Pike, is remarkably green and looks out of character against the Pennine backdrop. In fact these conical hills have more in common with the northern Lake District; they are composed of Skiddaw slate and stand aloof from the Cross Fell range.

The security of the track is soon left behind on the lower slopes of Scald Fell; the Way bears left **D**, continuing north as the track turns east. Ahead are Cross Fell and Great Dun Fell – the latter all too obvious because of the radar installation on its summit. The high fells still are some distance away.

After crossing a footbridge over boulder-strewn Swindale Beck, the Way begins a much sharper climb and takes a direct line north-east along an indistinct but cairned path **E**, parallel to an impressively steep-sided chasm carrying the upper reaches of the beck.

The next 1¼ miles (2 km) are of steady ascent, following an old hush up to Green fell spring. 'Hushes' are gashes in hill sides caused by mining activity; dams were constructed across natural clefts and the water released to scour the vegetation from the fellside and expose mineral deposits. Reference to a map reveals a jumble of several other odd words such as shake hole, cairn and currick. On the ground these features are less distinct. 'Shake holes' are conical depressions caused by underground subsidence and erosion of limestone. The word 'cairn', now universally employed to describe a pile of stones used as a

Contours are given in metres
The vertical interval is 10m

waymark for walkers, once referred to a mound of stones over an ancient burial site, while 'currick' was used for a pile of stones intended as a shepherd's viewpoint.

The long climb from cairn to cairn leads inexorably to Knock Old Man **27**, a great square obelisk of stones on the brow of Knock Fell overlooking the Eden Valley. The cairn provides some shelter from prevailing wind and rain (sunshine is unlikely to be a problem), but the top of the fell beckons and it is easy to push on, still heading north-east, to the summit cairn.

From here the Way changes direction and begins a north-west tack to link the major Pennine peaks. From the multi-cairned crown of Knock Fell **F** the route traverses rocky domes and drops down towards a road, with Great Dun Fell straight ahead. The small enclosure **28** marks a vegetation experiment undertaken by Natural England; from Swindale Beck in the south to the Tees in the north, and from Cow Green in the east to Hanging Shaw in the west, stretches Moor House National Nature Reserve. It is one of the most remote nature reserves in Britain and at first sight it is difficult to see why it is special, despite the presence of rare birds of prey and alpine flowers. In fact heather moorland and blanket bog are in short supply in western Europe: people come here from far and wide specially to enjoy the unique habitat and its severe climate. To the right of the path (north-east) lies a peaty plateau channelling water into the Trout Beck, which joins the Tees below the dwelling of Moor House. To the left **29** is one of several deep clefts in the Pennine ridge with exposed faces of limestone and whinstone.

At the tarmac road **G** the Way bears right and follows the road northwards for a short distance. The road leads to the radar installation topping Great Dun Fell, a white golf-ball with associated masts and buildings. It is easy to dwell on its negative aspects, which are inescapable. On the positive side, no one will ever get lost trying to find Great Dun Fell in anything short of white-out conditions. Also, aviation is safer for its presence.

The straight ascent of Great Dun Fell is barred by the near-vertical trench of Dunfell Hush **31**. The official Pennine Way route used to go to the north-east, but it now follows a much more sensible line, **H** north-west, splitting the angle between the road and the track, heading for the left edge of the radar station and above the head of the hush. Aim to reach the summit of Great Dun Fell to the right (east) of the radar station.

Contours are given in metres
The vertical interval is 10m

63

Cross Fell still dominates the northern skyline, but Little Dun Fell **32** is now visible in the foreground, an imposing and clear-cut land form more significant than it looks on a map and irresistible to any ridge walker. The Way heads directly for it, sweeping downhill to a marshy saddle **I** on a stone-slabbed path then climbing smartly to the open summit.

From Little Dun Fell the view back is disappointing, but this is more than compensated for by the prospect of Cross Fell, which now takes on goliath proportions. It is the highest point on the Pennines, and from here it looks it. From the scatter of boulders on the collar of Little Dun Fell's summit, the Way drops directly again to another saddle or link in the chain. A drop of rain falling here may flow either east or west – east to Tees Head **33** and the catchment of the Tees and so to the North Sea at Middlesbrough, west to the Crowdundle Beck and via the Eden and Solway to the Irish Sea.

Peat hags and black puddles used to make crossing the head waters unpleasant, but there is now a clapper bridge. The acidic flushes around Cross Fell boast several interesting but obscure plants. One of these is the alpine foxtail grass which has the distinction of being found in only a few places in northern Britain and nowhere else in Europe. The nearest neighbouring locality is Greenland. Limestone crags in these fells harbour more showy plants, such as roseroot and mossy saxifrage.

After negotiating the hags, the Way climbs steadily up a mainly stone-slabbed path **J**, heading straight up to the summit plateau rather than obliquely left as indicated on most maps. For several months each year fields of snow have to be traversed, and breasting the steep ice-shattered screes to reach the tall cairns on the edge of Cross Fell's table-top **K** is like stepping back into post-glacial Britain.

The surface of the plateau is stony and covered with short grass. *The Gentleman's Magazine* of 1747 describes the place as having 'a venerable aspect from the moss . . . and this can hardly draw a subsistence . . . so inconceivably barren is this distinguished eminence'. In many ways the summit resembles the Cairngorms and like this Scottish wilderness it is sometimes visited by mountain birds such as the dotterel.

Cross Fell triangulation point **34** stands at a height of 2,930 feet (893 metres). Nearby is a cross-shaped wind shelter which is remarkably effective in providing a temporary respite. Although it may have taken two-thirds of the day to get one-third of the distance, the remainder of the section is easy and a few minutes' rest and contemplation are in order. On a clear day the distant views are impressive, but such days are unusual; in the words of the 1747 magazine, Cross Fell is 'generally ten months buried in snow and eleven in clouds'. It can be an evil place and was known as 'Fiend's Fell' until recent times. Christians may have tamed the title but the landscape is still pagan.

From the shelter the Way heads north-north-west from cairn to cairn, and descends via Crossfell Well towards a well-worn track **L**. The views to the north, over the headwaters of the

As the Way approaches Alston it runs beside the South Tyne.

Black Burn, are wonderfully bleak. Once there would have been lead mines to catch the eye; now a sea of open moorland drifts to the far horizon with hardly a point of focus. The Way turns right to follow the track **35** – a very old Pennine crossing linking Garrigill with Kirkland, reputed (on rather flimsy evidence) to have been used to transport bodies for burial. This 'Corpse Road' provides an excellent, though hard, walking surface and the Way takes full advantage of it. After heading east-north-east beneath the impressive sweep of Cross Fell's north face, and past Greg's Hut **36** – an emergency overnight shelter with very basic facilities – the track turns north-north-east. The Way keeps with this all the way to Garrigill. Moorland lies all around. Sometimes the track passes old mine workings and its surface is strewn with 'gangue' – waste materials which include fluorspar. Pebbles or chips of fluorspar glow deep purple when wet, but they dry pale and opaque. Here and there pieces of galena (lead ore) can be picked up. These make good souvenirs but seem to get heavier and heavier through the day.

The walk along the Corpse Road continues for several miles. In general there are few remarkable features, merely a gradual increase in heather as the old mine workings and rough sheep walks give way to grouse moorland. Through a gate **M** the Way bears right then drops downhill to meet a wall **N**. The

Contours are given in metres
The vertical interval is 10m

route continues through another gate **O**, then with walls on either side, descends steeply past a Methodist chapel **P** and left along the road to Garrigill. As elsewhere on the moorland, this area has a number of walled tracks which were intended to prevent sheep straying when they were being driven down from the open fell to farms in the valley.

The little village of Garrigill **37** (the name is derived from Gerard's Gill – gill being an old Norse word for a narrow valley) is clustered around a village green, but it has little else in common with the bucolic atmosphere of Dufton; it stands in a cleft forged by the South Tyne River and its traditions are of the North-east.

The Way heads north-west along the main street but once out of the village, where the road bears uphill to the left, a stile **Q** leads right and parallel to the river. After a poor start – the South Tyne suffers from rubbish dumps and old spoil heaps – this riverside walk is attractive and full of interest, but at the end of an upland walk it is difficult to adjust your senses and appreciate the scent of ramsons in the alder groves or the piping calls of oystercatchers and sandpipers darting hither and thither along the river gravels.

Garrigill is an interesting little village, well worth a pause.

Contours are given in metres
The vertical interval is 10m

69

Eventually the Way crosses the river at a footbridge **R** and continues along the north bank, but after a step-stile by a gate **S** it bears right, obliquely uphill to Bleagate **T**. It then follows a line well above the river, mostly over pasture, along a well-signed and stiled path. If it is evening the sun will be setting over the high ridge linking Black Fell and Grey Nag in the west. The hills may seem to go on for ever, but this trackless wilderness, from Hartside to Cold Fell, is the reprise of the Pennines and what lies further north is the Whin Sill and the Cheviots.

The walk into Alston is completed along a firm, well-trodden path above a steep tree-shaded bank – a local beauty spot called the Firs **38**. Meeting dog-walkers and courting couples forces a rapid acclimatisation; it is you, not they, who have landed from outer space.

Alston

The little market town of Alston **39** wears a workaday face. Anyone driving across the Pennines from Hexham to Penrith, taking in the fine views along the A686, will be aware of a prosaic interlude of workshops and garages rather than the main town uphill to the east. The Pennine Way also does the town a disservice by sidestepping it and keeping to the South Tyne; it is only after several hundred yards that a view east over the river suggests there is more to the place than a shop-stop or bed and breakfast opportunity.

Alston is built close to the confluence of the Nent and the South Tyne. Houses, churches, schools and shops jostle for space on the rising ground. Although there are obvious signs of recent expansion, the core of the town is intact; on a bright sunny day Alston has the air of a hilltop village in Andalusia or Catalonia and should be explored in the same relaxed way. Even on the other 364 days of icy winds or misty drizzle it is worth walking up the cobbled main street from Town Foot, detouring past the Market Cross to the Butts or around Back o' the Burn to Town Head. Most of the buildings have a history, but there has been little effort over the years to make them picturesque. Cars and vans are parked at random, anywhere and everywhere, and there always seem to be signs and hoardings on the pavements warning of roadworks or advertising fish and chips.

Alston is disarmingly honest about itself. It seems at first glance to be based around the needs of the local farming community, and is reputed to be the highest market town in

A689 Melmerby
14 km or 8½ miles

Contours are given in metres
The vertical interval is 10m

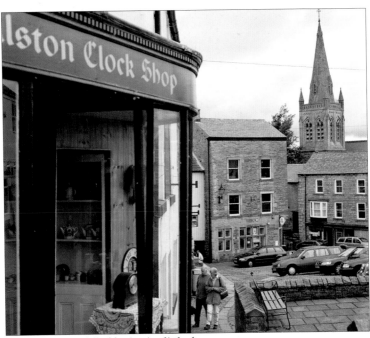

Alston is a town full of fascinating little shops.

England (Buxton in Derbyshire shares the claim). In fact its roots go very much deeper, into the hills where silver was mined at least into medieval times; and lead became a pervasive industry in the 18th and 19th centuries.

Alston was part of a royal estate leased to the king of Scotland in the 12th century but then held by the canons of Hexham Abbey until the Dissolution of the monasteries in the 16th century. For some years the developing village belonged to the Radcliffe family who lived at Dilston Hall a few miles east of Hexham. Some of the oldest surviving buildings, both manor houses and cottages, were built at this time and several carry 17th-century date marks. The older town terraces have stone steps leading to a first-floor doorway. When the town began to expand the houses were easily split into sub-units with their own entrances. Thus Alston became a bustling little settlement of tall square houses, with a wide cobbled market place where people could meet and barter, bet, bait or brawl. The Butts, an area of alleyways behind St Augustine's Church, was used for archery when long-bow practice was compulsory, before the reign of Henry VIII. Nearby, just down from the church, stands The Angel Inn, which dates back to 1614.

The Radcliffe connection came to a disastrous end when James Radcliffe, third Earl of Derwentwater and the illegitimate son of Charles II, joined James Stuart in the 1715 Rebellion. He was captured after the Battle of Preston and was executed in 1716. His brother Charles suffered a similar fate after the 1745 Rebellion. Alston became part of the Greenwich Hospital Estate and its associated mines were leased to the London Lead Company. When Dilston Hall was demolished, its clock and bell were given to the town; the workings have recently been restored and can be seen in St Augustine's Church. The hands are original but the face is a cunning fibreglass replica!

Most of present-day Alston town centre was built around 1800 when lead mining was flourishing. During the 19th century the place seemed to have a golden future. A short walk through the main streets at that time would have passed the Low Market and the busy High Market in front of the Crown Hotel; a slaughterhouse, a Wesleyan chapel and a Quaker meeting house; a grammar school, and a forge powered by a 14-foot overshot waterwheel. At the bottom of the town, on the road to Hexham, a railway station was opened in 1828 after plans for a narrow-gauge line had been approved by George Stephenson. Everything, except perhaps the climate, seemed to be set fair. Unfortunately the lead industry floundered in a few short years and Alston was stunned into a long and painful silence. Agriculture has kept the town going – just. Today there are signs of a revival and it is fascinating to see how the original mills and chapels have been transformed into engineering works, private dwellings, gift shops and galleries. However, because there has been no clear trend or development since the turn of the century, and no major rebuilding within the old heart of the town, there are much clearer links with the past. There are still rusting enamel signs advertising Oxo and the *Daily Telegraph*. One of the shops manages to combine selling old glass bottles and lamps with fresh fruit and vegetables. Half close your eyes and the delivery vans and cars could be wagons and pack ponies; the farmers and storekeepers talk in much the same way as they ever did. Conversely, with a few coats of paint, brushed-up stone work and appropriate street furniture, the market place could grace the cover of a holiday brochure.

The abiding charm of Alston lies in the fact that it has not quite become a tourist town. Certainly, the climate is against it. It lies in the heart of a cold land and its future, like its past, is tied to the Pennines.

Alston from the Pennine Way above the west bank of the South Tyne.

4 Alston to Greenhead

through Slaggyford and past Lambley Viaduct
16¹/₂ miles (25.7 km)

Some days are roses, others are thorns. If there is a disappoint-ment on any section of the Pennine Way it is likely to be the long walk from Alston through Slaggyford and by Lambley to Greenhead. The sections to the south and north, the high Pennine Fells and Hadrian's Wall respectively, are spectacular. This linking section has few highlights other than the Roman associations of the Maiden Way and the great wilderness of Blenkinsopp Common.

Alston **39** rarely seems to get up early and the chances are that you will be crossing the A686 road bridge **A** well before anything is stirring at the market end of town. This encourages a smug satisfaction, soon to be dashed as you get into the coun-try and see shepherds returning from the fells for breakfast.

The Pennine Way is signposted just after a right turn **B** where the A689 Slaggyford road angles north from the main A686 Penrith road. It begins as a driveway or track, then becomes a narrow path with the river and town to the right (east) and a field rising to moorland on the left. This path continues along the edge of a pasture through the old gates of Harbut Lodge **C**.

The climb north-west from Wanwoood leads to Whiteley Castle, a Roman fort built to defend the Maiden Way in the days of Agricola.

Contours are given in metres
The vertical interval is 10m

There is a detour at the lodge, to the left between buildings rather than past the front of the main house; this takes you around a small field past the coach house and over a step-stile on to a track **D**. The track leads up to the A689 and the Way then turns right (north) along this, before veering left (west) across a marshy field and through a gate to the right of an old barn **40**. The byre and barn have very old narrow glass windows and a stone-slabbed roof – features no longer appropriate to modern farming. White paint around the byre door was there so that cattle, and bleary-eyed milkmaids, could find their way in at pre-dawn milking time.

Just after the gate there is a little stream or sike, colonised by brooklime, a kind of speedwell with little blue flowers. The fleshy foliage is edible but univiting – particularly in sheep country where liver-fluke, which spends part of its lifecycle in water-snails, is endemic. Beyond the stream the Way heads uphill over pasture, leading to a ladder-stile over a wall **E**. The route used to do a curious loop south-west at this point to avoid a field with a bull in it, but this anomaly is now ancient history. The Way then crosses the marshy pasture to the north-west, then drops straight down to the footbridge **F** and so enters Northumberland. From here the route climbs by a very muddy path, crossing a stile and heading uphill **G** to meet a track and bear left (north-west) through improved pasture and out on to the open fellside.

Follow the track around the grassy ramparts of Whitley Castle **41**, a Roman fort built to defend a road linking the Stanegate at Carvoran with Watling Street at Kirkby Thore. Known as the Maiden Way, this road was probably laid about AD 80, after Agricola had blazed a trail northwards to crush the barbarians (see page 95). It is fascinating to see how drystone walls cut straight across the fort as if it were not there; for centuries farmers, and the rest of society, had a total disdain for history and apparently worthless relics.

At Castle Nook **H** the path avoids the farm by crossing the burn and heading down to the road. This road is the A689 of course; the Way flirts or plays hide and seek with it all the way to Lambley, until it turns west at Halton Lea Gate.

Across the road and through a gate there is a path on the right side of a wall which leads to Dyke House **I**, at which the route clips the corner of an enclosure around a group of houses. It then regains the same line north-north-west along the top of the fields, with a wall to the left and the narrow-gauge South Tynedale Railway to the right. At a gate where the wall ends **J** the route is obscure but goes straight on, across rough grassland to Kirkhaugh at which a tarmac track is followed left. After a group of buildings on the right, and well before the little Wesleyan chapel **42**, the Way turns right **K** and heads north-north-west in a straight line, across fields and stiles heading just to the left of the knoll of Lintley Farm **L**, then drops down to cross a footbridge over Thornhope Burn. The deep cleft of the burn has forced the trees to grow very tall; they compete at each other's expense to reach the light and make the streamside, and the five-arched viaduct **43**, a dark and damp place. Such places, with nooks and crannies in the old masonry, provide roosting sites for bats, such as the pipistrelle and long-eared. Nearby, the trees are the territory of the bigger noctule bat.

Nine viaducts were built to carry the Alston branch of the Newcastle–Carlisle railway. The line was built in the early 1850s, mainly to transport galena (lead ore) from the local mines to Haltwhistle and thence to Tyneside. It was never a

Contours are given in metres
The vertical interval is 10m

79

Midsummer – late June – is usually the best time for wild flowers.

successful venture; by the 1880s lead production had slumped, though about 20,000 tons of coal from the Tindale Fell Colliery (west of Halton Lea Gate) kept the rolling stock occupied. For most of this century the line has been uneconomic and in 1976 it closed for good. The section between Alston and Kirkhaugh has been reopened as a narrow-gauge steam line for tourists; the route of the old track is also a trail managed by Sustrans. The Way bears north-east around a field, following the bend of the Thornhope Burn, to meet the South Tyne again. The far bank of the river rises sharply through larch plantation and walled pastures, enclosed in the land-grabbing of the 18th and 19th centuries. Above, the heather is topped by Wardley Law at 1,552 feet (464 metres).

The South Tyne is restful rather than spectacular, and except in winter spate it rarely carries a great volume of water. It is usually wide, shallow and pebbly. A little way along the path you are introduced to this river in a delightful setting of riverside pasture, tumbledown walls and a bower of greenery. A pretty snapshot is marred by rubbish dumped along the far bank, creating an unfortunate impression of desecration; at the next bridge **M** the Way bears left to a road and forsakes the river, which is never seen at close quarters again. The road is the A689, following the old track of the Maiden Way and leading into the village of Slaggyford **44** ('slaggy' means 'muddy').

It is remarkable how many times authors on the Pennine Way nominate a Methodist chapel as a landmark or start point. Clearly, they were built at important places, and it is difficult to avoid them. From Slaggyford the Way leaves the third chapel of the day, leading down a track to its right **N**. This is a damp, deceptive track and botanical knowledge is useful; past hawthorn and ash trees all is well but a willow warns of wet ground – and so it proves as the track is hijacked by a little stream. Beyond this the Way dries out again through birch and hazel, then drops down to the Knar Burn and a blue footbridge, with a good view of another viaduct **45**. After this the Way crosses under the old railway line and then continues along a track to Merry Knowe **O**, detouring to the right, over a stile and around the buildings.

Contours are given in metres
The vertical interval is 10m

After following a wall for a short distance the Way crosses it at another stile and heads over pastureland, then crosses a road and makes its way over pasture again towards another viaduct **46**. Just before this a path bears right, down to a road, which is followed left across the Thinhope Burn until a path and then a track leads up past Burnstones and, via a spoil heap **P**, arrives at last on open moorland. The panorama is excellent. Glendue Fell is to the left (west), part of an extensive block of moorland including the RSPB reserve at Geltsdale. To the north-east, across the wooded South Tyne Valley, Wallace's Crags stand out on Ashholme Common. To the south is the Cross Fell range.

Underfoot is the Maiden Way, well-defined. At last you really feel you are walking with Agricola's army. A wet foot soldier would have known that Carvoran and the comfort of the Tyne Valley were not so very far away but would probably have heard nasty stories about what lay beyond in the border wastes.

The Way keeps to the very edge of the moorland and soon drops down to renew its affair with the A689, then crosses an attractive stream, the Glendue Burn, before rising again to follow a fence along the moor edge of Lambley Common beside the Maiden Way. This is a much wetter stretch. Grouse abound but there is also a high density of curlews and golden plovers and a good chance of seeing merlins or other birds of prey. Lambley, with its fine nine-arched viaduct **47**, lies in the valley to the north-east, but the north now beckons as the ridge of the Whin Sill, last seen in Teesdale, appears to the north-east, beyond the Tyne Gap.

The Way keeps to the east side of the fence on the plateau, then crosses it on the descent **Q** to the A689 west of Lambley village. Here it turns sharp west, then bears north down to the road, midway between the villages of Halton Lea Gate and Lambley.

CIRCULAR WALK: LAMBLEY AND THE SOUTH TYNE TRAIL

6 miles (9.5 km) (see map opposite)

This is an easy walk. Park at Lambley village and walk down a wooded path to Lambley viaduct, then south along the course of the old South Tyne railway line to link with the moorland section of the Pennine Way described more fully at the top of this page.

Contours are given in metres
The vertical interval is 10m

The Pennines are a good place to see the beautiful, rare and, sadly, persecuted hen harrier – the male notable for its predominantly powder-grey plumage.

The Way follows a stone-flagged path over boggy ground. Make for a grassy knoll, then for a low stone marker on the brow of the hill, then continue north-north-west to High House **R**, a ruined barn. From here descend along a grassy spur to cross the Hartley Burn at a blue bridge. For a little while the path keeps to the burn side, by alders and downy birches, before striking uphill to cut off the corner of the pasture, with Foxhole Cleugh to the west. The path is now across farmland, from stile to stile through pastures and the steading of Batey Shield, then down to a foot-bridge over the Kellah Burn and a side road and up a track to Greenriggs. The only problems are likely to be around the farm steadings, particularly at Greenriggs **S** where it is important to follow the route through the gate to the left (west) rather than the right (east) of the house.

This leads to another gate, after which the Way climbs north-west up a field to a ladder-stile **T** before a near-featureless block of moorland. This is Hartleyburn Common, leading to the even more daunting expanse of Blenkinsopp Common. A wet desert of hair-moss and coarse grasses drifts away in all directions; sheep have a hungry look, birds are few and silent. Walk north-west, heading a little to the left (west) of the brow of Round Hill **U**. From here bear right and head north or north-west for $1^1/_2$ miles (2 km) across rolling ground. The Pennine Way is distinct in most places but is unreliable. There are a few walls and fences, otherwise waves of wind-scorched grass stretch like dunes to the horizon. At the end of a long day such a prospect

Contours are given in metres
The vertical interval is 10m

85

may not lift the spirits, but a wilderness is always worthy of respect. Eventually a triangulation point appears on the skyline at Black Hill **V**. Make for a point to the right of this, after which the A69 Tyne–Carlisle road will be visible below.

This is a busy and dangerous road: cars are eager to overtake lorries on this stretch, and the Way avoids the hazard by dropping down to Gap Shields **W**. It then follows a muddy track through a gate, and detours south-east along a track under pylons, to ruined buildings and mine workings **X**. It then heads downhill and back under pylons before meeting the road half a mile west of Greenhead village **48**. For those continuing the walk, the Way crosses the road directly and leads up to a steep bank **Y**, then heads north-east and east across fields to meet the B6318, Gilsland Road. The quickest way into Greenhead, for facilities or overnight accommodation, is to follow the course of the old road, past Banktop and down Greenhead Bank.

Contours are given in metres
The vertical interval is 10m

Birds of prey

Birds often help us to fix a memory of place in our minds; kitti-wakes above a windswept cliff, turtle doves along a dusty southern lane. In the Pennines, the call of a golden plover or curlew can stir the spirit of a walker, but it is the sighting of a hawk or falcon that sends the heart racing.

Britain's birds of prey were decimated in the 18th and 19th centuries by gamekeepers. The only exception was the kestrel, a hovering mouse-killer never seen as a threat to pheasant or grouse and therefore ignored. In the 1950s an additional hazard, pesticides, wreaked havoc even among falcons nesting in remote and forgotten uplands, and changes in agriculture were beginning to reduce the suitable hunting territories. When the Pennine Way was established it might have been possible to walk the whole route without seeing a bird of prey at all. Now, it would take very bad luck or bad observation not to encounter one or two, even if only as nameless shadows over distant hills. However, even the briefest of sightings should provide a few clues to identification and a worthwhile memory to take away.

The commonest bird of prey in most uplands is the spar-rowhawk, which nests in shelterbelts or forest plantations but ranges widely in search of food. The male is quite small and feeds on finch-sized birds; the female is much larger and takes anything up to pigeons and jackdaws. Sparrowhawks have broad brunt wings and a bullet-shaped body; they are usually seen flying very fast along hedges, hoping to take prey by sur-prise, but sometimes they soar high over their territories, cir-cling like miniature eagles.

In some places where there are extensive and mature conifer plantations, such as in north Derbyshire and south Northumberland, goshawks occur. These look like giant spar-rowhawks and have similar hunting habits, but they are rare and elusive and have only recently become established after vir-tual extermination. A sighting on the Pennine Way would be fortunate indeed. Buzzards, by contrast, are among the easiest of birds of prey to locate; they are very big, enjoy soaring over open valleys and hillsides, and have a loud 'mewing' call. Again, trees are necessary for nesting, but in this case the requirement is for broadleaved woodland, and the bird is most common where there are relics or fragments of oakwoods on the sides of steep valleys, as there are above the Eden in Cumbria. In general, buzzards are increasing, but lack of habitat and continued keepering is preventing them from colonising most of Yorkshire and Northumberland.

Buzzards have a wingspan of up to 5 feet (1.5 metres). The only other long-winged bird of prey of comparable size likely to be seen over the Pennines is the hen harrier. At any time of the year wide expanses of open moorland may attract lone hen harriers. Their habit of quartering low over the ground, wings held in a shallow V, makes them easy to identify. The male is gull-grey with black wing-tips; the female and juvenile birds (much more likely to be seen here than adult males) are brown with a white rump. Pairs of harriers select young conifer plantations in which to nest, but they need large expanses of open hunting territory nearby and the Pennines are not particularly favoured. Persecution by gamekeepers is still one of the major problems.

Most walkers in the Pennines who see large birds of prey search among the pictures of hawks or buzzards in their field guides, but they would be better served looking among the owls, for it is the short-eared owl that is most likely to come to their attention. This is partly because it hunts methodically over a regular patch and is therefore easy to see, and partly because in most years it is tolerably common. The short-eared owl feeds on voles and its breeding success is dictated by the abundance of its prey, which means that it often has a bumper breeding surge followed by a disastrous crash. One year there are owls everywhere, the next year none.

Short-eared owls choose similar habitats to hen harriers both for nesting and hunting, which means the two species are often seen over the same block of moorland. However, the moth-like flight of the owl is quite unlike that of a hawk and its wings are broad and seem pale against evening heather. Unlike other owls the short-eared often hunts in broad daylight, especially if it is hungry or has a nestful of owlets to feed, but it is most often encountered in the early evening, silent as a ghost.

Finally, on the Pennines there are the falcons. These are sharp-winged and agile predators; even the kestrel, which nests as readily on crags as on trees, seems to enjoy the freedom of the open fells and has a dashing and purposeful flight. Most Pennine Way walkers hope to see merlins and peregrines but have to be content with kestrels. Fortunately, after many years of decline, a reduction in the use of toxic chemicals has resulted in a spectacular increase in the numbers of peregrines and many long-deserted crags have begun to echo to the 'kek-kek-kek' of nesting birds. Peregrines often stay close to their crags all year but they are free spirits and can turn up almost anywhere. The peregrine has a wingspan of over 3 feet (1 metre) and has a barrel-chest and broad wing-bases, yet its power is tempered by effortless grace and in flight it is easily the most impressive of Pennine birds. By contrast, the merlin is mercurial; it kills its prey by a chase rather than the hammer-blow of a stoop and its flight is low and very fast. It nests among heather or in low stunted pines but needs tracts of undisturbed moorland over which to hunt – hence it has become a rarity, even in the North Pennines. The male is grey and not much bigger than a large thrush, the female is brown and a little smaller than a kestrel.

Few places offer as good a chance of seeing birds of prey as the Pennines. Apart from the species that nest regularly along the route of the Way, there is always the chance of a migrant – a hobby, osprey, rough-legged buzzard or kite. The sky is a high-way for such creatures and the Pennines are no barrier to them.

Open country north of Hareshaw House. Heather and moor-grass, rocky outcrops and conifers: ideal habitat for birds of prey like merlin, goshawk and peregrine.

5 Greenhead to Steel Rigg

by Hadrian's Wall
6¹/₂ miles (10.6 km)

If you are in a hurry this section can be walked in less than three hours, but life is too short not to use each day more wisely. Hadrian's Wall requires contemplation, and in any case the country through which it passes is more tiring than it looks. Give it a whole day and it will repay you in spectacular memories. On the other hand, if it is raining the exposed ridge upon which the Wall is perched is a misery. Pity the Romans, who knew it all too well. 'O me miserum' might have been etched into every stone.

Starting on the B6318, the Gilsland road north out of Greenhead **48**, the Way begins as a track beside a terrace of red-brick houses, then crosses a railway line and the Pow Charney Burn **A**. It then arcs northwards to follow the larger Tipalt Burn round a field to Thirlwall Castle **49** and Duffenfoot. Without realising it you are already well into the stuff of history and legend, for the Wall once ran west–east across this field and the Pennine Way crosses its buried foundations just south of the castle. The flat ground marks a gap in the natural barrier of the ridge and was therefore a weak point in the Roman defences. It is here that Caledonian tribesmen are thought to have broken through, possibly during the Barbarian Conspiracy of 367.

Thirlwall Castle, a fortified tower-house dating back nearly 700 years, was built from stone dismantled from the Wall and the nearby Roman fort of Carvoran. Few people could afford to care about their historical heritage in the benighted Middle Ages. Edward I stayed here on 20 September 1306, during his wars against the Scots, and its menacing walls must then have seemed an oasis in a desert of squalid border poverty. But its heyday was brief. It has been in ruins for at least 300 years but has recently been conserved and consolidated by the National Park Authority.

The Pennine Way turns right in front of the castle mound, down to a footbridge where it crosses the Tipalt, then goes through a gate and passes Holmhead **B**, then climbs uphill through woodland along a walled track. At the end of this there is open pasture and the Way follows a wide, grassy ditch beside a wall. The ditch **50** was part of the Roman fortifications and ran along the northern side of the Wall. Another broad ditch called the Vallum marked the extent of the military zone to the south.

At the brow of the hill the Way enters Northumberland National Park and crosses a ladder-stile, continuing eastwards with a wall to the right. Beyond this is the unexcavated Agricolan fort of Carvoran **51**, beside the museum of the Roman Army. Dominating the view eastwards is Walltown Quarry **52** – once an ugly scar but recently transformed by the National Park Authority. On the far brow, Hadrian's Wall can be seen for the first time **53**. If the grey cliffs look familiar it is because they are part of the Whin Sill, last encountered along the Pennine Way in Teesdale, and, as in Teesdale, several quarries worked the dolerite for roadstone. This serpent-backed ridge is known as the Nine Nicks of Thirlwall, but quarries have altered the silhouette and made the name less appropriate.

The Way meets a road and turns right along it, then turns left into Walltown Quarry, now a picnic area with a small café, a lake and useful facilities like a toilet block. The route exits the quarry via a kissing wicket-gate. It then heads north-west along the top of the quarry face, directly to Hadrian's Wall.

Contours are given in metres
The vertical interval is 10m

5 km or 3 miles
A69 Haltwhistle

A vivid imagination is essential to see the Wall in its original glory, for nowhere is it even half complete. However, the setting helps to create a suitable atmosphere, and this should be an exciting moment. Walking eastwards, the Way shares the route of the Hadrian's Wall National Trail and takes you along the crest of the Sill with the steep scarp slope, colonised by rowan, birch and aspen, to your left and the gentle dip slope to the right. The soil is quite thin and in places plates of whinstone are exposed. The deep fissures in these grey pavements are often green with moss and there are patches of wild chives – a rare plant said to have been introduced by the Romans.

The Wall itself, after a fine turret (44B) **54** standing up to 10 courses high, dwindles to a few fragments or the ghost of a mound often topped by an ordinary drystone wall. The original Pennine Way follows the Military Way, a supply road, but it is better now to follow the new Hadrian's Wall Path, if only for the views north, across wastes and mires to Wark Forest.

Aesica (Great Chesters) Roman fort **55** comes as a surprise – most people find themselves walking through the middle of it

Contours are given in metres
The vertical interval is 10m

before they notice anything unusual. This and the total lack of information signs make it a refreshing place. Most of the Wall forts, including Aesica, post-date the first phase of building (the original idea here had been for a smaller milecastle) but they were written into the plans when it was found that the older forts of Vindolanda and Carvoran were too far away to allow for the necessary rapid deployment of troops.

From Great Chesters, the Way drops down, past a stone cottage **E** and over a stone stile on to the road, across the Caw Burn, then right into Cawfields Quarry **E**, an attractive picnic site with toilets and interpretive panels **56**. Once past the large pond, and a fine cross-section of the Whin Sill **57**, which shows the cooling pattern of the volcanic rock, a path climbs back to the ridge crest and passes the stone skeleton of Milecastle 42 **58**, with an excellent stretch of the Vallum visible at the foot of the dip slope to the right **59**.

The subsequent walk along Cawfield Crags takes you along one of the best-preserved sections of Hadrian's Wall, much of it having been renovated in the last century. After Caw Gap **F** it

Contours are given in metres
The vertical interval is 10m

is possible to get into a good stride along Windshields Crag to reach the highest point on the Whin Sill **60**. On a clear day you can see south across the Pennines, west over the Solway Firth, and north to the Cheviots (Cheviot is the whaleback to the left, Hedgehope the more conical hill to the right). The word 'shield' or 'shiel', in many local place names, is a leftover from the days when farmers spent the summer with their flocks, staying in huts out on the hills.

From the triangulation point at 1,132 feet (345 metres) the Way quickly descends eastwards to meet a side road **G**, then the Steel Rigg car park **61**. If you intend overnighting at or near the Once Brewed Youth Hostel you can follow the Military Way to meet the side road a little further down the hill **H**, and turn down this to the main road, known as the Military Road or Wade's Road because it was built by General Wade to carry troops. The youth hostel has the National Park Visitor Centre to the east, and The Twice Brewed Inn to the west.

CIRCULAR WALK: HADRIAN'S WALL AND WALLTOWN

5¹/₄ miles (8.5 km) (see map on pages 91–92)

Park along the B6318 where it crosses the Pennine Way north of Greenhead. From here, follow the way past Thirlwall Castle through Walltown Quarry and briefly along Hadrian's Wall, turning south after Walltown Farm and then west through wet moorland and pastures to return via Greenhead. For easier parking, an alternative starting point would be at the car park at the old Walltown Quarry **52**.

CIRCULAR WALK: HADRIAN'S WALL AND ONCE BREWED

5 miles (8 km) (see map on page 94)

Park at the Once Brewed Visitor Centre and walk along the waymarked route through fields to the south of the B6318 (the Military Road). After crossing the line of the Stanegate Roman road, the walk crosses the B6318 and makes for Hadrian's Wall, from where it turns east along the Pennine Way along the high section of the Whin Sill. (For this last section, see the route description at the top of page 94).

The Romans

What would British history have been like without the Romans? Did the invasion of Claudius in AD 43 mark the end of an idyllic pastoral economy or the beginning of true civilisation? Perhaps both. Relics of the occupation once littered the country, but over the centuries the scars have healed. Only in the far north, especially across the rolling hills between the Tyne and the Tweed, are there clear signs of their endeavours. The Pennine Way acts as a transect to the remains and offers a unique insight into what it might have felt like to walk for days and arrive in a wilderness.

Agricola's army reached the North Pennines and Cheviot Hills in AD 80–81. By establishing a network of roads defended by forts and supply bases, the legions were able to push further north into Caledonian territory and leave isolated pockets of resistance to be mopped up later. Many impressive Iron Age forts, visible today as rings of tumbled stones circling the tops of rounded Cheviot foothills, were bypassed in this way and were

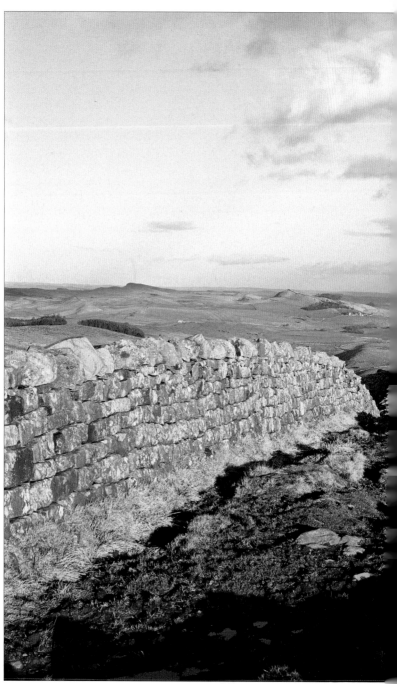

Hadrian's Wall follows the crest of the Whin Sill, reaching its highest point here at Whins[

s. In the distance is Crag Lough.

then starved into submission. Woden Law (see page 134), just north of the Border Ridge, bears the marks of siege equipment on the grassy slopes next to its hill fort, and it seems likely that the site was later used for soldiers or legionaries to practise siege tactics. Dere Street, the Roman road from York to what is now Edinburgh, passed close by and is visible today as a green track crossing the Border at a wooden gate. A few hundred yards downhill to the south is the immense complex of marching camps called Chew Green, while on the ridge crest by Brownhart Law there is a Roman signal station. In those faraway days this area would still have had some tree cover and would not have seemed so remote. It is difficult now to imagine the busy activity of the Roman occupation; all that remain are a few ghostly lines on the hillside. A wasteland has been created on what was once the gateway to a new civilisation.

The arterial roads on either side of the Pennines were linked at the Tyne–Solway Gap by an important lateral route called the Stanegate, and forts (constructed of wood) were built at Carvoran (see page 91) and Vindolanda. Agricola led his army deep into Caledonia to control the Forth–Clyde isthmus and fought a successful battle at Mons Graupius, but never pushed on into the Highlands. Perhaps he thought that his task was complete. When he retired to Rome the British tribes seemed to have been subdued, particularly the Votadini of the Border area. But trouble eventually flared and the Romans were obliged to withdraw once more to the Stanegate. This occurred about the year AD 100, in the reign of the Emperor Trajan. In 117 Trajan was succeeded by Hadrian, whose first concern in the north was the failure of the Stanegate system, which was allowing raiding tribesmen to terrorise the northern province. Hadrian had seen active service in Upper Germany where walls of turf had proved effective barriers, and he may have heard about the Great Wall of China. Whatever his inspiration, he settled on the idea of building a wall to protect the boundary of his Empire. In 122 he visited Britain to oversee the project; he was a fit man and enjoyed walking, so it is tempting to imagine him striding along the great whinridge recommending the line the defences should take.

This project kept the legions gainfully employed for eight years. The plans were changed several times, but the final system comprised a wall 80 Roman miles long (73 English miles / 117 km), stretching from Bowness in Cumbria to Wallsend near Newcastle. West of the River Irthing the Wall was built of turf, but to the east it was built of sandstone blocks, requiring 1.3 million cubic yards

(1 million cubic metres) of stone, not to mention lime for mortar and whinstone rubble for infill. When it was complete the wall stood 16 feet (5 metres) high at the foot of its ramparts and was 6 1/2–10 feet (2–3 metres) thick.

The old Stanegate forts were augmented by new forts along the line of the Wall, 12 altogether, and between these there were milecastles and turrets. To the north of the Wall lay a V-shaped ditch, while to the south was the Vallum, a wide ditch with high banks, marking the extent of a military zone.

Today the finest remains of the Wall follow the crest of the Whin Sill in Northumberland National Park; the route of the Pennine Way includes the most dramatic viewpoints and the remains of two forts, Great Chesters and Housesteads, on its sidestep along the north brow of the Tyne Gap.

Places to visit, close to the route of the Way, include Carvoran (Museum of the Roman Army), Once Brewed Visitor Centre (run by the National Park), Vindolanda and Housesteads. Of these, Vindolanda has a superb collection of finds from excavations, while Housesteads enjoys the most dramatic setting.

In its heyday the Wall system was serviced by 10,000 troops, mostly auxiliary soldiers from across the Empire. The logistics and infrastructure required to keep the operations going were considerable. Villages grew up around the forts and for miles around farmers were obliged to grow wheat to feed the garrison.

The Wall remained as the frontier of the Empire for nearly 300 years. Although there were long periods of peace there were also episodes of violent conflict. A 'Barbarian Conspiracy' in 367 overwhelmed the defences completely and for a while there was total anarchy. Eventually, in 410, the local population (by now part-Roman through intermarriage and trade) was told that it would have to defend itself. The Empire began to evaporate. Britain was on her own again and entering a Dark Age over which the mists of time have drawn a heavy veil.

Although there are many Roman remains in the south of England, the associations seem stronger in the north, where the power of the Empire was so severely tested. Along the Pennine Way people walk in the footsteps of Agricola, Hadrian, Severus and Count Theodosius. There are inscribed stones, ramparts and ruins to be discovered in many unexpected places, and of course there is the Wall, of which the most dramatic fragments survive along the Whin Sill between Walltown and Sewingshields. Civilisations may come and go but the rocks remain.

6 Steel Rigg to Bellingham

past Crag Lough and Lowstead
14³/₄ miles (23.7 km)

The most dramatic start to any section of the Pennine Way begins from the National Park car park at Steel Rigg **61**. Within a few minutes you are walking beside the Wall, taking a well-trodden path alongside the broad, consolidated remains of Britain's most important ancient monument. The Wall didn't look quite like this in the days of the Romans; it was much higher then, but you certainly have a clear sense of history 'close at hand'. The switchback crest of the Whin Sill lies ahead, its steep north-facing scarp looking out over frost-shattered scree and the rolling 'cuesta' landscape towards the forests of Henshaw Common. Away to the south, across the Tyne Gap, are the Pennine moors of Whitfield and Cold Fell. This is a fascinating and threatening place. It must have seemed like the end of the world to the Romans, and it can be cold and windswept even in high summer.

The Way keeps close company beside the wall (it used to run along the top!). The gap in the line of the Whin Sill before Peel Crags affords a good view of the grey face of quartz-dolerite, squeezed out as magma between beds of limestone and sandstone nearly 300 million years ago, then cooled and weathered into near-hexagonal columns. Below the rock face is a rubble of scree **62** colonised by such plants as parsley fern and club moss.

Peel Crags sets you into a good walking stride before dipping down into Castle Nick and Sycamore Gap, sharp clefts in the Sill created by Ice Age meltwater. The National Trust and National Park Authority have been doing a great deal of restoration work in this area, involving temporary diversions to the Pennine Way, and both the Wall and Milecastle 39 **63** are in good shape. The loose stonework provides nesting sites for wheatears with their distinctive black-tipped tail and white rump. The name 'wheatear', which might seem inappropriate considering the habitat, began as a down-to-earth description, 'white-arse', but was cleaned up in Victorian times. The path over Highshield Crags, above Crag Lough **64**, runs on the north side of a wall (not The Wall, which is missing here), and close to the edge of the Whin Sill. Vertical chasms in the rock face add a hint of danger and should be negotiated with care.

The view of the lough is excellent. There are usually swans on the water, either whooper or mute depending on the time of year. Other wildfowl look very tiny from this height. The path, dry and firm underfoot, drops down through a plantation of pine, wych elm and sycamore, then leads out on to a track with the marshy eastern edge of the lough, colonised by willow, alder and birch, just to the left (north). Turn right, following the track through a gate **A**, then immediately leave the track and cross a ladder-stile to the left. There is now a rather steep pull, past the grass-covered remains of Milecastle 38 and Hotbank Farm **B**, up to Hotbank Crags. The Wall is again in good order and very imposing. Four lakes are visible from here. Away to the south-east is Grindon Lough, one of the best birdwatching places in the area (lots of wild geese, occasional hen harriers, peregrines and merlins), while north of the Wall there is Crag Lough (to the west), Greenlee Lough **65** (to the

Contours are given in metres
The vertical interval is 10m

north) and Broomlee Lough **66** (to the north-east). All these lakes are shallow and occupy basins created in the Ice Age when ice sheets creaked eastwards, scouring out depressions in the bedrock. The fate of these attractive lakes is to become bogs; some old maps show Caw Lough **67**, this side of Greenlee, as open water, but nothing is now visible. In Roman times the wilderness north of the Wall must have been a land of lakes.

At Rapishaw Gap **C** the Pennine Way leaves Hadrian's Wall, thus depriving you of the most famous Wall view, towards Cuddy's Crags, and the finest excavated fort at Housesteads (Vercovicium) **68**. Is a detour recommended? On balance, no. It is a long way to Bellingham and there is always another day for sightseeing.

Released from the Wall, the Way heads north-north-east over marshy ground. The view back is a little disappointing, the crags not so dramatic and Housesteads barely visible on the dip slope. To the east the Sill rises to Sewingshields Crags (where King Arthur and his knights are supposed to be sleeping), then drops away like a spent wave on the shore of Tynedale. Ridley Common provides an unexpected interlude of heather and a pretty burn **69**, then the Way drops at Cragend to another burn

Contours are given in metres
The vertical interval is 10m

102

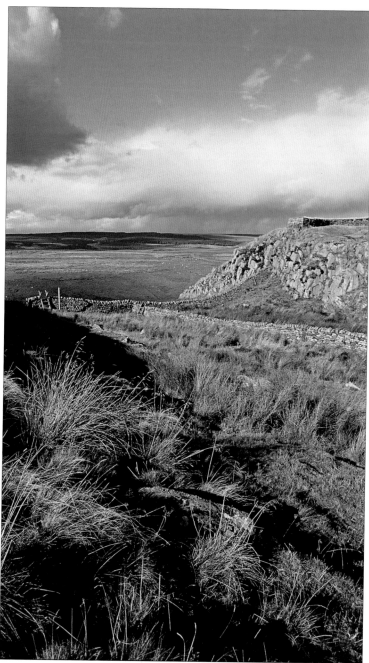

Rapishaw Gap is the natural cleft in the Whin Sill between Hotbank Crags and Cuddy's Crags.

Contours are given in metres
The vertical interval is 10m

104

Contours are given in metres
The vertical interval is 10m

with a footbridge **D**. After this the path arcs eastwards, but it is indistinct and easily lost. Make for the forest to the north, with Greenlee Lough now visible to the west. Pass to the east of East Stonefolds **E**, then enter Wark Forest along a wide drive. The Way gains height steadily through the forest, along the drive then right along a path which leads out eventually at a step-stile and gate **F**.

This block of moorland, edged on three sides by spruce forest, has an eerie stillness about it, even on windy days. To the west is Bellcrag Flow, to the south is the heather-clad brow of Hawk Side **70**. Harriers probably gave the place its name. Across the sea of wet moorgrass, make for the small group of stunted pines **G**. These lie within a winged sheepfold, so shaped to afford shelter from any gale. This makes an acceptable stopping point for lunch, though the desolation of the place may cause you to hasten on your way. A little to the east of where the Way re-enters the forest **H** there is a standing stone called Comyn's Cross **71**. Legend has it that the sons of King Arthur heard that their father had given a gold cup to a local chieftian, Comyn (or 'Cumming'), on his visit to Sewingshields. They rode forth to retrieve the gift, and slew the chieftain at this point.

From the stile leading back into the forest the prospect of Sitka and Norway spruce does not appeal, but a few steps further on there is a fine vista of more varied woodland, improved by the informal presence of larch. The Way leads down, crossing four tracks or drives and heading at first towards Ladyhill Farm **I**, then bearing to the west in line with Willowbog Farm **J** to lead out on a side road between Stonehaugh and the B6320.

After a short road walk the Way turns northwards again along a forest track **K**, through spruce plantations, crossing two tarmac drives, before leading out to grassy moorland. The Way forms the boundary of Northumberland National Park between Ladyhill Farm and Bellingham, but route-finding may be difficult as wall-lines on the map do not correspond with what you see on the ground. Bear to the left of the brow of Ground Rigg **L**, then left down between hillocks, keeping to the upper right bank above Fawlee Sike (a 'sike' is a small stream).

If you have judged the route accurately you will find yourself beside a beautiful little waterfall **72**, a vertical cascade of up to 20 feet (6 metres), overhung with rowan, ivy and heather, with a misty basin of moss-covered rocks and shelves of hart's tongue and hard fern. A delightful spot and quite unexpected.

From here, follow the line of an old dyke or sod-cast ridge – the ghost of an enclosure hedge – crossing wet drainage channels by detouring to the left until eventually the Way leads over a ladder-stile across a wall, then downhill with grassy dykes to either side and towards the Warks Burn. A sharp right turn **M** through a gate and past a haybarn will bring you within sight of a footbridge **N**. The rock-lined Warks Burn lies in a deep, shady cleft. It is a pretty, birch-lined stream making its way eastwards to join the North Tyne below Wark village. The height of the cliff may not seem very terrifying but a few hundred yards upstream at Low Roses Bower there is a loo (or 'netty') corbelled over a 43-foot (13-metre) vertical drop, reputed to be the greatest in Britain. This uncomfortable prospect must have strengthened a few constitutions in its time, but the house has been derelict for years.

Once on the far bank of the burn, green pastures begin to dominate, and one small farm leads to another. Route-finding is straightforward but needs care around farm buildings, where there might be signposted alternatives. Horneystead **73** dates back to 1837 and lies adjacent to the ruin of a fortified bastel-house built about 1600 (see page 144). The Ash **74** is 18th–19th century, with an elaborate Victorian conservatory or porch. Leadgate, on the side road to Wark, is of similar vintage. By far the most intriguing of the farms in the area is Lowstead **75**, perched over the east bank of the Blacka Burn. Around the little yard are grouped byres, stables and a cart shed and granary. The house, with its diamond-paned windows, and the adjoining byre to the left, are bastel-houses dating back to the 16th century. The 4-foot (1.2-metre) thick walls would have allowed the farmer and his family to sleep secure from 'reiving, riding Scots'.

Contours are given in metres
The vertical interval is 10m

107

A little way down the track above the Blacka Burn in Linacres, a modern, large, functional farm screened by tall trees. The Way follows the track eastwards **O**, then meets a road and follows this north-north-east, past a small quarry and limekiln on the left **76**. The hilly, close-cropped pasture on either side of the road is spectacularly 'cord-rigged', a mosaic of field systems dating back to Roman times. The uneven ground in the field corner marked on the map as a 'homestead' **77** (see page 109) was excavated in 1960 and revealed a typical Romano-British settlement comprising a rectangular enclosure and several circular stone huts. The fields all around were under cultivation to provide barley for the occupying garrison of the Wall forts. The land was farmed for at least 300 years, from the Iron Age to the fall of Rome, after which came the Dark Ages and a shadowy reshaping of society.

Where the road meets a T-junction **P** the Way continues north-east as a field path, alongside a fence and the remnants of a thorn hedge. After crossing the lines of three old sod-cast field boundaries the path heads downhill to cross the Houxty Burn at a footbridge **Q**, just downstream of Esp Mill. Once on the far

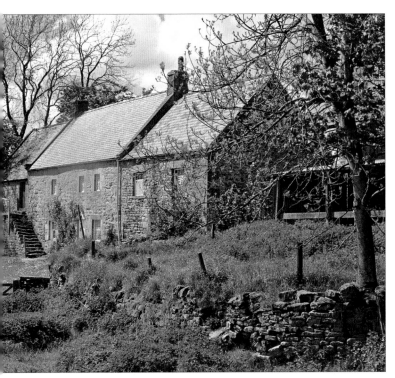

Lowstead has evolved from bastel-houses built in the days of Border conflict to protect the inhabitants from rustlers and thieves. The buildings have recently been renovated.

Contours are given in metres
The vertical interval is 10m

3 km or 2 miles
Walk

bank and past Shitlington Hall **R** (names can be misleading – it's only a farmhouse) the Way heads along a track, then uphill beside open pasture, before climbing up the sandstone edge of Shitlington Crag and finally reaches a ladder-stile **S** in the wall to the left (west) of the tall radio mast. Beyond is a fine expanse of heather moorland on the crest of Ealingham Rigg, while to the south and south-west is a wonderful view of the route you have taken across the forgotten fields and forests to the north of the Wall.

After crossing the stile and walking along a track eastwards the Way suddenly heads out north-east across the rushy moorland **T** to make for a marker post on the brow of the hill, then, after crossing level ground, drops down again into the North Tyne Valley. The views of Bellingham, and the next section of the route, would round the day off nicely but there is an uncomfortable road walk remaining. The River North Tyne may deflect some of your irritation. It is a handsome river and is at its best between Bellingham and Wark. The old ford at Bridgeford **78** used to be the only all-year crossing, but the 'new' bridge **79** (built in the 1830s to replace one washed away in the Middle Ages) provides a suitable viewpoint. After crossing the bridge, turn right down the steps to the recreation ground. Follow the path along the river bank. Turn left past Cuddy's Well and continue behind the town hall into the square **80**.

Rivers and burns

What happens to all the rain that falls on the Northumberland hills? Some of it certainly ends up in the boots of walkers but most of it is absorbed into a layer of peat and bog-moss. The water gradually seeps downhill through the blanket bog and gathers into narrow channels or 'sikes', which then run into streams or burns.

Most of the rivers with headwaters along the Northumberland stretch of the Pennine Way, such as the Coquet and the Aln, flow eastwards to meet the North Sea, but after the last Ice Age the course of the North Tyne was deflected southwards, to capture the Rede and the Warks Burn which had probably fed into the Wansbeck. The North Tyne now meets the South Tyne near Hexham, then flows east to Newcastle and Tynemouth.

There are few natural lakes within sight of the Pennine Way, and these are small and diminishing each year as they are choked by bog-moss and carr or willow/alder scrub; the lakes or loughs (pronounced 'loffs') of the Hadrian's Wall area lie in

Quarries (dis)
Reenes
Leo House
Blakelaw Plantation
West Reenes
Old Len's House
Blakelaw
The Riding and remains of Bastle
Fernwood
Workings (disused)
White Hill
Reenes Quarry (disused)
Waterfall
Whitley Well
Bogglehole Cottage
Mine Workings (disused)
Greenhead
CH
Caravan Park
Resr
Dodd Heaps
Bellingham
123
134
Fair Stead
Copseford
The Shaws
80
FB
114
Hotel
P
T H Pol Sta
115
Sheep Pens
79
Cuddy's Well
Bridge Plantation
Schs
Dunterley
Border County Ride
Riding Stone
83
Sewage Works
Deerwood
121
Brown Rigg
Cemy
The Mill
Brown Rigg
Mill Haughs
Appley Peth
Eals Burn
River North Tyne
Boat Farm
Forestry Commission District Office
Reservoir
Kings Wood
Eals
78
Eals Haugh
igg Common
Quarries (dis)
Bridgeford Gate Cottage
Sheep Dip
82
Starks Cleugh
Settlement
Fell End
T
Spr
241
Ealingham Rigg
Quarry (dis)
Chapel Well
Pit (dis)
S
Blind Well
Relay Station
Pennine Way
wood
81
Shitlington Crags
Kittyshield Sike
Sheepfold
West Ealingham
Shitlington Crag
Ford
Quarry (dis)
Shieldfield
Blinkbonny Cottage
Bastle (remains of)
132
R
83
Shitlington Hall
Temple Green
84

Contours are given in metres
The vertical interval is 10m

B6320 Wark
5 km or 3 miles

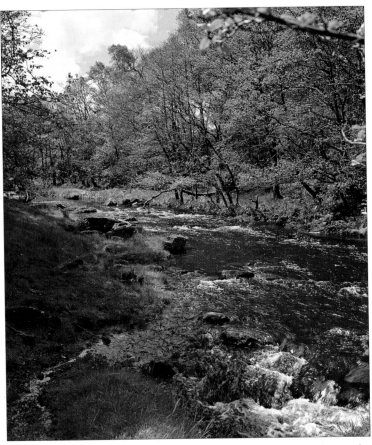

Warks Burn rises in the uplands of Northumberland National Park and meets the North Tyne below Wark village.

the basins hollowed out by moving ice and they are shallow and reed-lined. Their visual impact in such a stark and stony landscape is considerable.

The gradient from the hilltops to the coast is quite steep, so once rainwater has filtered its way through marshy grassland and blanket bog into sikes and runnels, it tumbles quickly down well-defined rocky burns and sometimes cuts deep rocky gorges, as in the Warks Burn and the Hauxty Burn south of Bellingham. Water derived from rain soaking through the spongy layer of peat is acidic and the bedrock is mostly sandstone or andesite. This means the upland burns are poor in dissolved nutrients, though they are cold and turbulent and therefore rich in oxygen. These factors, together with the problem of coping with winter spates and summer droughts, mean that wildlife has to be well adapted. One of the most characterstic plants of stony riversides is the monkey flower, which originates from California, while the upper, shady banks of rivers often have patches of the beautiful melancholy thistle and giant bell-flower. In some places, especially on the South Tyne where there has been contamination by heavy metals from lead mining activities, riverside grassland contains extensive patches of the mountain pansy.

Among the mammals, the water vole is uncommon but the otter, which has disappeared from most of England due to the effects of toxic chemicals and habitat destruction, is still widespread here. The North Tyne is one of the best rivers in the country for otters, as it is for salmon and sea trout.

The number of waterside birds decreases with altitude. Along the lower reaches of the larger burns there are sand martins, common sandpipers, oystercatchers and herons, and also goosanders, which were first recorded as British breeding birds on the River Coquet in the 1950s and are now found throughout Northumberland. Nesting birds of the rocky and turbulent upper reaches are limited to dippers and grey wagtails, and a few intrepid mallards.

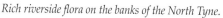

Rich riverside flora on the banks of the North Tyne.

Shitlington Crag lies on the Way to the south of Bellingham.

7 Bellingham to Byrness

via Whitley Pike and Brownrigg Head
14³/₄ miles (23.7 km)

Bellingham **80** (pronounced 'Bellinjum') is a grey little town of 1,000 souls. Among the shops and inns there is a 13th-century church of St Cuthbert, with an unusual stone-slabbed roof, constructed centuries ago to replace previous ones burned down in Scottish raids (see page 143). There is also a memorial in the market square **81** to local heroes who fell in the Boer War and, nearby, a curious mounted gun called a gingall, brought back from the Boxer rebellion in China.

From the centre of Bellingham the Pennine Way follows the West Woodburn road, downhill and across a bridge **A** over Hareshaw Burn. There is a reminder, in the shape of a signpost, that the route continues along the road. A track alongside the burn and through a National Park car park leads to Hareshaw Dene **82**, a beautiful valley clothed in ancient wych elms and oaks. The route once took this course to allow a visit to Hareshaw Linn, one of the most attractive waterfalls in the country. Common sense dictates the diversion, relegating the Dene to an optional extra, perfect for an evening stroll but impossible to enjoy as an early detour before a long day.

Just after the bridge over Hareshaw Burn is the old course of the Border Counties railway line **83**, constructed in the 1850s and 1860s to carry coal and iron ore. It was never profitable; once the industries had gone the line relied upon passengers and farm stock. The axe finally fell in 1956.

Uphill out of the town, the Way at last leaves tarmac **B**, heading north when the road goes east. The rounded mounds east of the junction are spoil heaps **84**, weathered green by the years, grass having formed a callus over the scarred landscape. Iron from the Hareshaw Iron Company furnaces was used in the construction of the High Level Bridge in Newcastle, but the enterprise was short-lived, opening in 1838 and closing just 10 years later.

Up the farm road, the wooded cleft of Hareshaw Dene is visible across the fields to the west. The Way eventually turns through the middle of Blakelaw farmyard **C**, past a lovely jumble of old and new buildings: stone troughs, pigsties, farrowing crates and gathering pens, asbestos and metal sheds and painted woodwork.

On the other side, with a lime kiln in the field away to the north-east, the Way gains height up an open grassy hillside, to an isolated post, then past the corner of a stone wall **D** and over the grass-decked spoil of old coal workings. On the sky-line there is a pine plantation; to the right (east) of this is a stone ruin **E** and the gate that leads the Way back on to high moorland.

Boulders among the grass just beyond the gate have been colonised by some fine lichens, most notably *Peltigera*, a large, foliose ('leaf-shaped') species, but as the path leads downhill and back into Northumberland National Park the vegetation changes to rushes and moss.

Contours are given in metres
The vertical interval is 10m

6 km or 3½ miles
B6320 Wark

The Way forks here **F**, the official route making for the higher ground with Callerhues Crag to the east **85** (an alternative route keeps to the lower ground, until it meets the main route west of Hareshaw House **86**).

North of the farmyard the Way continues along a wide track **87**, the ghost of a small coal-carrying railway line, past a quarry and workings and out on to the B6320 (west to Bellingham, east to the A68 and Otterburn). The Pennine Way crosses directly, north-north-east past an old mine and its spoil heap **88**. The circular stone enclosure away to the west pre-dates any industrial relics and is a kind of sheepfold, called a 'stell'.

The ground rises steadily, from mat-grass to heather, and there are few obvious landmarks except for grouse butts **G**. Head towards the grouse butts, following the defined track through the heather as it bears north-east, then north-west.

Hareshaw Linn lies at the head of a beautiful tree-lined valley.

Grouse Butts

Ninewell
Eyes

W

336

Great Moor

Curricks

Wetshaw Hope

Lough
Shaw

G

BS

Grouse Butts

Currick

Wetshaw
Well

Sheep

89

295

Pennine Way

BS

320

White Rigg

304

B6320 Otterburn
6 km or 3½ miles

Sheepfold

Sheepfold

88

Rowantree Linn
(Waterfall)

Brockley Burn

Waterfall

r's Sike

ndysike
Bog

247

Quarry
(dis)

88

87

Meg's Moss

 O6320

Sandy Sike

87

262

ers Cottage

Sheepfold

Black Sike

Sheepfold

nden Hill

86

Sheepfold

Hareshaw Burn

Haining rigg Burn

84

The Shanks

FB

Linn Well

Hareshaw Linn
(Waterfall)

Trough
Wr Twr

309

Hareshaw
Head

BS

310

330

Sheepfold

340

BS

BS

Abbey Rigg

326

Quarry
(dis)

Quarries
(dis)

Hareshaw House

86

Hazel Burn

Sheepfold

Air Shaft

Sheepfold

Percy's Mos

Berry Crag

343

323

Cairn

340

Callerhues Crag

85

Matthew's Quarry
(disused)

The Pikes

Sheepfold

Callerhues Moss

Spr

Sheepfold

Little Callerhues
Crag

School Crag

F

85

Sheepfolds

Highste

249

Workings
(dis)

Quar
(d

Currick

Contours are given in metres
The vertical interval is 10m

119

Rough pasture and open moorland west of Padon Hill.

The hill is Deer Play **89**, a wide wilderness with limitless views. Perhaps red deer were once hunted here, but they have certainly all gone now. By way of contrast, roe deer have thrived because of the increase in forest plantations and can often be seen, but not usually very far from cover. A stone post **H** provides a good stopping place for lunch, after which the route descends north-west, rising by an indistinct path to the cone of Whitley Pike **90**.

Once on the summit of this hill the route heads north-west, straight downhill on a stone-slabbed path across marshy ground, making for a cattle grid and gates over an unfenced road **I**.

Route-finding is much easier now as the Way follows a fence for several miles. As the fence leads north-west on the straight forward ascent of Padon Hill there is a large sandstone boulder **91**, its surface heavily weathered. Bronze Age inhabitants of these hills often carved 'cup and ring' marks on to such stones,

120

but so far nobody has claimed that any of the sculpted marks on the Grey Mare rock are anything other than natural. However, the summit of Padon Hill bears a very obvious man-made feature, a bell-shaped tumulus **92** built in the 1920s by the Morrison-Bell family who once owned nearby Otterburn Hall. Most of the stones used for the cairn would already have been on the hilltop; Padon Hill got its name from Alexander Peden, a Scottish Presbyterian who held services in out-of-the-way places. This was during the reign of Charles II when Nonconformists, especially Scots, were repressed. Local people attending the illicit gatherings were requested to carry a stone with them up the hill to add to a growing symbol of defiance.

Contours are given in metres
The vertical interval is 10m

Emperor moth – one of the biggest insects of heather moorland. The male flies in spring sunshine; the female spends most of her time hiding in the heather.

The Way passes to the west of the brow of the hill, but a stile over the fence allows access to the 'pepperpot' cairn and provides excellent views over Redesdale. Due east is Otterburn, and just to the north of the village is the site of the Battle of Otterburn, fought in 1388 between the Scots and the English, at which the Earl Douglas of Scotland was killed and Sir Henry Percy ('Harry Hotspur', son of the Duke of Northumberland) was captured. The story of the battle – a Scottish victory – is told in a ballad popularised by Sir Walter Scott.

From Padon Hill the route keeps to the fence, with heather all around. The block of moorland always has a high population of emperor moths. This beautiful creature, the only British member of the silk moth family, is on the wing on sunny days in April and May. The massive caterpillar, green with black bands and covered with short bristles, is seen in late summer. It feeds on heather but enjoys sunning itself on the bare ground, where it either intrigues or terrifies walkers.

The Way drops down to a marshy saddle **J**, then rises via a steep little ascent to Brownrigg Head **93**. There are fine views north-east to the Cheviot massif, and south to Padon Hill, but ominous plantations of spruce trees begin to make an impact on the landscape; to the north-west stretch many miles of the Kielder complex of Forestry Enterprise land, while the steading of Gib Shiel to the west has become encircled by a private forest plantation. For some distance the Way continues with forest on one side and open moorland on the other. Occasional stones bearing the letters GH set the bounds on the old Redesdale estate of Gabriel Hall, High Sheriff of Northumberland in 1705.

Contours are given in metres
The vertical interval is 10m

Eventually the route arcs westwards and becomes enclosed by trees. The twilight world of Kielder is entered at Rookengate **94**. Most walkers feel a sense of foreboding at this point. The notice somehow makes this worse; perhaps it should quote Dante: 'All hope abandon, ye who enter here'.

Once through the gate and on the wide forest drive, things do not seem quite so bad; the ground is firm and any wind and weather is elevated to the treetops. Vistas along rides reveal high hills to the north and moorland to the east, and there is a constant twitter of birds – mostly coaltits and chaffinches, but also crossbills. There is a chance of seeing sparrowhawks or even goshawks, predators which benefit from the seclusion of the forest.

The only constant features are the main drives and the little stone bridge over Greymare Sike **K**; the trees come and go, *en masse*. After several miles the drive descends, the green pastures of Redesdale at last appearing through the trees to the

The way through the forest, north to Redesdale.

Contours are given in metres
The vertical interval is 10m

125

north-east. The farmstead is Blakehopeburnhaugh **95**, its buildings and land now owned by Forest Enterprise. The name has appeared in the *Guinness Book of Records* for many years as the longest place name in England. The elements are simply explained: 'Blake', black; 'hope', a fertile strip of valley land; 'burn', stream; 'haugh', low-lying land by a river. After miles of spruce plantations this is a pleasant and verdant place. The Blakehope Burn is peaty and handsome, and a little further on is a bridge **L** over the River Rede ('rede' means 'red', another reference to the colour of the water). According to most old Pennine Way maps the route passes uphill after the bridge, but in practice this is impossible and merely leads on to the busy A68 and a tedious road walk to Byrness. The real route keeps to the east bank of the Rede, along a riverside with deciduous trees towards Cottonshopeburnfoot, then across a bridge **M** to the west bank and continue along a forest track through a plantation before turning downhill **N**, across the Rede again and past a picnic site and the beautiful little Holy Trinity Church **96**.

Incidentally, recent maps show Cottonshopeburnfoot as one word where it used to be two – hence it should displace Blakehopeburnhaugh as the longest place name.

Byrness village **97** is a curious little settlement of terraces built by the Forestry Commission in the 1930s. It may lack style but it is a welcome sight and has all the necessities for tired walkers.

The Border Forest

Conifers have an honourable place in the northern landscape; juniper and pine were once more widespread here than oak and there was a time, before the last Ice Age, when Norway spruce was a true citizen of the hills. These days it is fashionable to view conifer plantations with contempt, which is to damn by association some of the most beautiful landscape features in Scotland and the Lake District. Unfortunately, it would take a miracle for the peaty-gley soil of Kielder to yield anything but pulp-mill fodder and the impression from the Pennine Way is of an unwholesome world of spindly trunks and gloomy shadows.

Kielder Forest was a panic response to timber shortages after the First World War. Blocks of spruce trees were planted across the whole landscape irrespective of contours, watercourses or hilltops. The Forestry Commission was charged with a simple economic remit which did not embrace such novel concepts as conservation. Over the last few years attitudes and economics have forced a change and the future is brighter; as the present even-aged forests reach maturity the age structure is being broken up and new plantations are being shaped around landscape features. Alder, birch and rowan trees are being planted along water courses and footpaths (but not the Pennine Way, yet) and Sites of Special Scientific Interest are now managed sensitively or have been handed over to conservation agencies. But the essential business of Forest Enterprise will always be to produce timber. Its 200 square miles (518 square km) of landholdings at Kielder produces 300,000 tons per year, most of it to be pulped for newsprint or shredded for chipboard. At present about 70 per cent of the forest is composed of Sitka spruce, with less than 5 per cent

Contours are given in metres
The vertical interval is 10m

The Forestry Commission village of Byrness with Catcleugh Reservoir to the north-we

broadleaf. But the proportion of 'native' broadleaf species is increasing as areas are clear-felled, and there is more emphasis on multi-purpose use of the forests. Conservation and access are the watchwords.

When planting began in 1926 it was anticipated that forest industries would employ thousands of people, so special villages of terraced houses were built at such places as Stonehaugh and Byrness. Mechanisation, and the invention of the chain saw, has resulted in a massive reduction in the workforce and most of the houses have now been sold or stand empty. Forest Enterprise at Kielder employs a staff of only about 170 people, although there are many subcontractors and associated industries which enhance the local economy.

One of the most damning criticisms of conifer plantations is that they are virtually lifeless. This is quite untrue in that there are always more birds and animals in an acre of forest than an

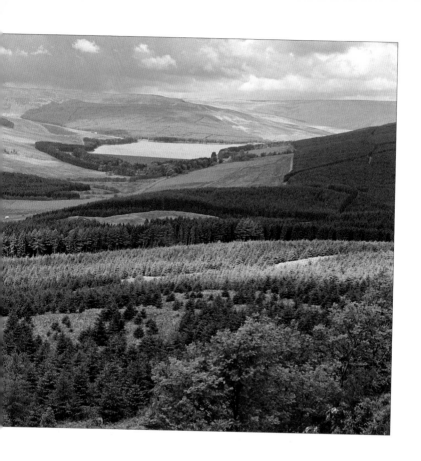

acre of moorland. However, chaffinches and goldcrests do not have the same charisma as golden plovers and merlins, and the moorland habitat is diminishing at an alarming rate. Among the animals to benefit from the forest are red squirrels – Kielder is one of the last English strongholds – roe deer and foxes, and there is a strong likelihood that wildcat and pine marten will soon be recolonising the Border hills via the forests. Young conifer plantations are excellent habitats for nesting birds, including short-eared owls and hen harriers, but mature spruce forests are poor; crossbills, which are common locally, and goshawks, which are rare, are the icing on a very dull cake.

Finally, it is worth remembering that Forest Enterprise does not have a monopoly on growing trees. Many existing plantations, in square regimental blocks, are the work of commercial forestry groups. It will be interesting to see how many of these survive to maturity.

8 Byrness to Clennell Street

past Chew Green and along The Street
13³/₄ miles (22 km)

The village of Byrness **97** was created for workers, first to build Catcleugh Reservoir, then to plant the Border Forest. As the trees of Kielder grew, the hamlet melted into the darkening forest. The number of foresters required to manage the plantations gradually decreased, so that several of the houses fell vacant or were sold. The recently converted youth hostel occupies a prime position in the stark terrace, while farm cottages and guesthouses provide alternative overnight accommodation. Byrness is a stopover on most all-the-way itineraries because it precedes the Cheviot traverse. To complete the walk to Yetholm in a final day of 27 miles (43 km) is hard; an alternative, followed for convenience in this book, is to be picked up by prior arrangement at Rowhope or drop down for an overnight stay in Coquetdale. There are additional access points at Chew Green (west by public road through Coquetdale or east along a private MOD road, often open to the public during the spring and summer), or by dropping down to the north of the Border Ridge along Clennell Street into Cocklawfoot.

The A68 is a notoriously fast and dangerous road. The Pennine Way crosses it from the Holy Trinity Church **96** by heading north-west alongside it for 50 yards then up a tarmac path to a gate beside Byrness Cottage **A**. From Byrness village a short road walk south-east, crossing to a wide tarmac drive, leads up to the same gate. From the gate cross a field, then go through another gate and across a forest drive, then head uphill on a path through a mixed conifer plantation. The path is steep and straight, an excellent start because it takes an uncompromising line and wastes no time in gaining height and leaving the forest behind. After a short scramble up a rock edge the brow of Byrness Hill is reached. The lower courses of a stone fire lookout tower and the concrete base of a hexagonal hut **98** show how useful this place has been for a view over the Border Forest. By turning your face to the north you are suddenly at the threshold of a very different world, an open ridge often hammered by wind and rain and leading to the loneliest of hills in the least-populated part of England.

The Way heads north-west, along the broad crest of the ridge, from Saughy Crag to Houx Hill **B**. To the west is the head

Contours are given in metres
The vertical interval is 10m

of Redesdale, culminating in the Border crossing at Carter Bar. Catcleugh Reservoir sparkles like whetted steel against the deep green of the surrounding forest. Built at the turn of the 20th century, when 1,000 workers were employed for 15 years, it still supplies Tyneside with water; nearby Kielder Water may be 20 times the size but it was surplus to requirements even before it was completed in 1982.

The next high point along the Way is Ravens Knowe **99**. Ravens no longer nest here – keepers and shepherds carry a heavy burden of responsibility. The word 'knowe' means 'hill' – usually not a very big one. 'Law', as in Emmet Law to the east, means much the same thing. The view from Ravens Knowe is excellent, especially to the east, across the basin of the Cottonshope Burn to Loan Edge. This is Ministry of Defence property and signs warn of the dangers of trespass. The message on some of the signs is simple: 'Do not touch anything. It may explode and kill you.' The MOD owns 20 per cent of Northumberland National Park, a paradox that has brought criticism and controversy ever since the Park was created in 1956. The path itself is completely safe, and the whole block of land north of the Coquet is now a 'dry training' area with no live ammunition, but inevitably one's impression of the place is blighted.

The Way keeps to the high ground, to Ogre Hill with Harden Edge to the east. It then descends over boggy ground to the Border fence, a well-worn path following the fence-line north-north-west with the official route to the east, and crosses a step-stile **C** into Scotland. Were it not for the forested slope of Ogre Hill this would be a featureless waste; the exact line of the Border is arbitrary, depending on where each generation of farmers has replaced the fence.

Once, the Pennine Way turned north-east here to follow the sodden flow of the Coquet's headwaters **100**, but now the path leads north for a few hundred yards, then forks right **D** to drop down obliquely and meet a wicket-gate **E** above the more clearly formed Coquet. There is a great reluctance to lose height so dearly earned, but the sacrifice is worthwhile as the route takes you around Chew Green **101**, a sprawling green maze of low earthworks marking Roman marching camps. The Pennine Way leads east, with the Coquet below and grass-covered ramparts above, then bears north-west around the edge of the earthworks. Coquetdale can now be seen as a steep-sided valley of interlocking spurs.

This is the only place on this section of the Way that is close to vehicle access. If you plan to leave the Way at this point and have arranged transport, go east at **F** along the 'escape route'. Cars can now drive right up to this point via Alwinton on the Coquetdale road. Alwinton itself is 12 miles (19 km) away. The ancient Gamel's Path **102** is now a military road to Redesdale Camp, and access is limited to those few days a year when the

Hindhope Law

Mid Hill

Border Co

405

Hind Hope

482

455

Sheepfold

391

394

ROMAN SIGNAL
STATION

103

470

Earthworks

Brownhart
Law

Dere Street

ROMAN ROAD

Shee

420

Earthwork

425

Berrystell Fell

Euro ER, Co Const, P Const & Per Bdy

09

G

439

Chew Sike

de Hill

436

Chew Edge

ROMAN CAMPS
& FORTLET

P

hwork

Chew
Green

101

Medieval Village
of Kemylpethe
(site of)

390

DANGER

E

F

08

D

Coquet Head

Pennine Way

Border County Ride

River Coquet

Sheepfolds

Ford

Co Const & CP Bdy

100

C

463

Dere Street

ROMAN ROAD
(course of)

102

508

521

Border County Ride

DANGER AREA

527

509

516

07

493

Harden Edge

Cross Cleugh

Sheepfold

Ogre Hill

Yard Shank

Sheepfolds

Canker Cleugh

470

450

DANGER

Fool Sike

Artillery Ran

400

Sheepfold

Emmet Law

Ravens Pike
(Cairn)

99

Ravens
Knowe

Sheepfe

DANGER AREA

Ravens
Crags

Sheepfold

06

349

78

79

Spr

Enclosure

Contours are given in metres
The vertical interval is 10m

133

red flags are not flying. If you are continuing on the Way, cut the corner at Chew Green and walk north uphill, alongside or among the ghosts of Roman billets and parade grounds. There is little left except the spirit of futility, of Shelley's 'Ozymandias' – 'Look on my works, ye Mighty and despair!' Chew Green was a stopover on a previous long-distance route, the perilous road from York to the Caledonian wilderness.

Halfway up the hill the Way bears north-east **G** to pick up the shadowy trackway that was Dere Street, and follows this to the Border fence to the north-east of Brownhart Law, close to a Roman signal station **103**. The Way stays with Agricola's road for a little longer, heading northwards along the Border Ridge. Rainwater falling on the Scottish side drains into Hindhope Burn, and thence into the Kale Water and the Teviot, which meets the Tweed at Kelso. Thus, west Scottish rain ends by flowing east to meet the North Sea at Berwick. Dere Street crosses the Border at a five-bar gate **104** and makes its way down to the Kale by skirting Gaisty Law, Hunthall Hill and Woden Law. The Pennine Way stays on the high ridge and makes for a mound with a peat-built cairn and a post **H**. A clear path then leads north, obliquely away from the Border fence arcing eastwards via stone cairns and posts, and across marshy ground with short boardwalks over sikes and burns. The vegetation is sparse, apparently lifeless and unappealing, but for centuries herds of wild goats have survived in the Cheviots, as far from civilisation as they can get. After the October rut they range down into the valleys searching for better grazing. How long the goats have been here is a mystery – perhaps they were introduced by the monks of Lindisfarne. Certainly the domestication of goats dates back to the New Bronze Age, and feral or semi-wild herds have been roaming this lonely range of hills for at least 1,000 years. Wild goats come in many shapes and sizes, but are most often grey. The billies are big, long-horned, long-haired and seedy-looking.

The Way crosses some very boggy ground at the head of Rennies Burn **I** and there are some curious basins of *Molinia* grass **105** looking like mouldy pink porridge and known to walkers as the 'Grassy Loughs'. *Molinia*, or purple moor grass, is inedible or unappetising to most livestock, and much of the afforestation in Northumberland, particularly in the area to the north of the Wall, has taken place on impoverished 'prairie land' because it is good for nothing else. However, on this open ridge the scenic quality of the grass is far more significant.

Contours are given in metres
The vertical interval is 10m

135

Back along the Border fence, now heading east, you start to notice the widening views, which are very fine. To the Scottish side are the fertile lowlands of the Teviot valley and Tweedsdale, the characteristic profile of the Eildon Hills by Melrose, and in the far distance the Lammermuir and Moorfoot Hills that bar the way to Edinburgh. On the English side the andesite foothills of the Cheviots obscure any view of the east coast.

At a fence corner the Way turns sharp left **J**, north-north-east, and drops down over tussocky grass to a gap in the Border Ridge called Yearning Saddle. A wooden shelter **106** is maintained here by the National Park Authority for the use of walkers, and it makes a welcome stopping place, out of the piercing wind.

The word 'Yearning', as in Yearning Law, the hill to the south-east, may be derived from the Anglo-Saxon word 'erne' meaning 'soarer', and applied especially to the white-tailed eagle. Golden eagles are occasionally seen over the Border hills and moors, but the white-tailed eagle was lost to Britain over 60 years ago and its reintroduction still hangs in the balance. There are other bird

The Border Ridge, from Lamb Hill to The Cheviot.

Contours are given in metres
The vertical interval is 10m

names among these hills: Gowkhope ('gowk' is cuckoo), Cushat Law ('cushat' is woodpigeon), Cocklaw ('cock' is woodcock), and Corbies Crag ('corbie' is carrion crow) are clear examples.

From Yearning Saddle and its view of 'The Kip' **107**, above Kipp Sike to the north-west, the Way follows the Border fence faithfully for several miles, deviating only to cut obvious corners. The ridge links a chain of high hills, including Lamb Hill, Beefstand and Mozie Law. From Beefstand **108** there is a classic view of the cold granite heart of the Cheviots, the wide whaleback of The Cheviot itself, flanked by Hedgehope and The

The climb from Coquetdale along The Street is one of the finest walks in the Cheviot Hills.

Schil. Mozie Law **109** is heathery with peat hags, the broad headwater allowing rainwater to seep south into the Coquet or north to Heatherhope Burn and its little reservoir. The route cuts off a fence corner before Plea Knowe **K**, then leaves the fence again to avoid a marshy patch called Foul Step (Pennine Way walkers were not the first to experience the blanket bog of the Cheviots; there are several other 'foul steps' in the area). Away to the south is a beautiful grassy ridge linking Black Braes to Swineside Law and Coquetdale. The clear track along the crest of the ridge is The Street **110**, an ancient drove road at its busiest before the Border troubles which started 700 years ago (see page 143). It is possible to follow this venerable green road down into Coquetdale to find accommodation at a farm or shepherd's cottage, but the total detour would be 6 miles (10 km) with a loss of at least 820 feet (250 metres) in height. Dire emergency would be the only reason for this course of action, though as part of a circular walk out of Coquetdale, from Windyhaugh, this path has distinct possibilities (see page 140).

Ahead now is Windy Gyle, one of the most elegant and enigmatic of the Cheviot summits at a very respectable 2,030 feet (619 metres). It has a steep, sweeping slope southwards to the Rowhope Burn, beyond which the main features are the conifer plantation of Carshope and the cairned dome of Thirl Moor.

The ascent of Windy Gyle is direct, straight up beside the English side of the fence. A stile **L** provides access to the hilltop, which is on the Scottish side. The route of the Way continues along the English side. The great Bronze Age mound of stones is called Russell's Cairn **111**.

To control the violence in what had become a buffer zone between kingdoms, the Border was split after the Middle Ages into three marches, each under the wardenship of a lord appointed by the king. There were regular meetings at remote Border crossing points between the corresponding wardens, but these sometimes degenerated into bloodbaths. The Hanging Stone on the slopes of Cairn Hill (see page 146) was used for such meetings, as was Russell's Cairn, where Lord Francis Russell was murdered at a wardens' meeting in 1585.

Desolate and often snow-swept, and with violent and sinister associations, Windy Gyle is one of the atmospheric highlights of the Pennine Way. It is, quite literally, miles from anywhere.

CIRCULAR WALK: THE STREET, AN ANCIENT DROVE ROAD ACROSS THE BORDER RIDGE

8¹/₂ miles (13.5 km) **(see maps on pages 139 and 141)**

This walk, which rewards a quite steep climb with wonderful views, starts near Windyhaugh (grid ref. 865110) on the upper reaches of the River Coquet. Drive to it from the B6341 (the Otterburn–Alnwick road) via Harbottle and Alwinton.

Park near Windyhaugh and follow the road alongside the river, leaving it soon after crossing Rowhope Burn to join a green uphill track. This is The Street **110** (see page 138), which takes you all the way up to the Border Ridge. From here, the route follows the Pennine Way eastwards to Windy Gyle (see route description on page 138 and above). Then, from the summit, leave the Way to return southwards along an indistinct grassy path descending all the way into Coquetdale at Windyhaugh.

Contours are given in metres
The vertical interval is 10m

141

From the shoulder of Windy Gyle the Way leads along the fence-line and descends quite sharply before levelling off at about 1,770 feet (540 metres). After half a mile another old drove road cuts across the ridge at a ladder-stile and gate **M**. This is Clennell Street, once the busiest of all the ancient Border crossings, which can be followed north-west to Cocklawfoot.

This is the logical halfway point on the Cheviot traverse and you should consider continuing only if you are feeling fit and there are at least six hours' daylight left.

Backpackers can overnight here to the lee of the ridge, but for the rest there is an unavoidable detour in order to find accommodation.

Contours are given in metres
The vertical interval is 10m

Border troubles

The barren state of the Border hills reflects a turbulent episode in Britain's history, beginning with an attack on Scotland by Edward I in 1295 and ending with the Union of the Crowns in 1603. Had this gloriously wild part of Britain never been a frontier, its agriculture would have developed further and faster.

Many armies have fought in the Borders – Romans, Normans, Celts and Anglo-Saxons – but between major conflicts there were long periods of peace during which the rural economy was able to recover. However, the troubles that began in the 14th century rumbled on for too long for anyone to feel secure, and war became a fact of life. Both the land and the people grew impoverished and mean; only the most powerful landowners were able to protect themselves, by building tower-houses with massively thick walls. Thirlwall Castle (see page 90) dates from this period.

The most famous Border battle took place in 1388 when Earl Douglas of Scotland gained a victory over the impetuous Harry Hotspur, son of the Earl of Northumberland, in a moonlit encounter on the hill above Otterburn in Redesdale (see page 122). Hotspur gained his revenge in 1402 at the battle of Humbleton Hill in the Cheviots, where he was able to employ Welsh archers to decimate a Scottish army 10,000 strong.

After the division of the Border area into marches, and the violence associated with this (see page 140), the whole area degenerated into a wasteland. Any remaining vestige of tree cover disappeared, houses were burned to the ground, cattle were stolen and whole families killed by marauding 'rievers' or 'mosstroopers'. The worst areas for the lawlessness were Redesdale and Tynedale on the English side, where the residents were accused of being 'wild and misdemeaned people' who delighted in 'theftes and spoyles'.

Not surprisingly, landowners continued to build their houses with thick walls and call their tenants to the muster roll at the first sign of trouble. 'Pele towers', smaller versions of the tower-houses, were widespread by the end of the 15th century – for those who could afford them. One of the best-preserved examples, of a 'vicar's pele', is at Elsdon in Redesdale. In 1555 a defensive zone 20 miles (32 km) wide was established right along the Border, and the inhabitants of the area were obliged to dig ditches to keep out the 'reiving, riding Scots'. Poor farmers built turf cottages which could easily be rebuilt; those with

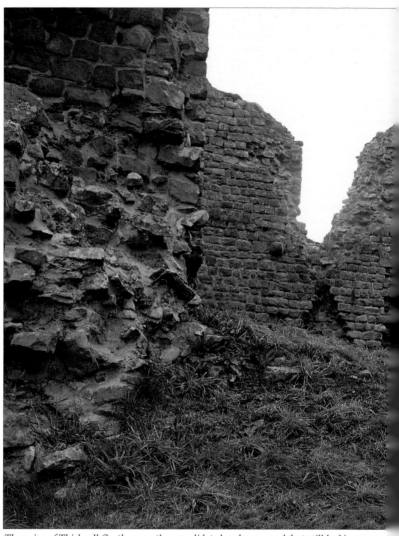

The ruins of Thirlwall Castle, recently consolidated and conserved, but still looking precar

something worth defending built square bastel-houses. These dour grey buildings had walls 3 feet thick and tiny windows. The ground floor was probably used to house cattle and sheep, while the upper floor, accessible only by a heavy trapdoor, provided living quarters for the family.

The worst of the troubles came to an end as a result of the Union of the Crowns in 1603 and the Restoration in 1660. People began to look forward with hope, though new farmhouses were

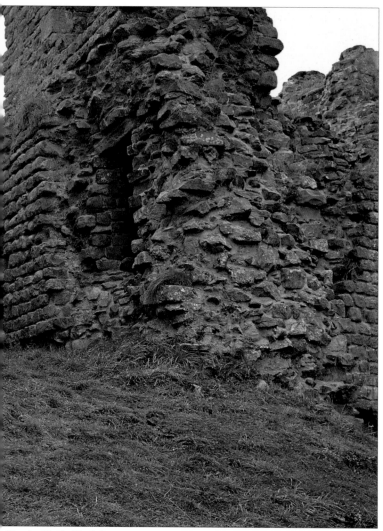

...illtop beside the Tipalt Burn.

built solid and square, reflecting a lack of trust in human nature and the weather. Old bastels fell derelict, as at Horneystead (see page 106), or were adapted and used as barns or byres, as at Lowstead (see page 106).

It has taken more than 300 years for the Borderlands to recover from the bitter harvest of war. The wide hills and valleys of Northumberland still bear the scars.

9 Clennell Street to Kirk Yetholm

past The Cheviot and over The Schil
11¹/₄ miles (18 km)

The Pennine Way embraces some of the best scenery in the Cheviots, and traversing the highest ground has now been made easy by recent management work, including the advent of stone slabs. This section begins at the Border Gate, a dip in the ridge east of Windy Gyle, marking the crossing point of the ancient trackway of Clennell Street **112**. It is reached by walking the Border Ridge, on the Pennine Way, or by climbing from Usway Burn and Coquetdale to the south, or from Cocklawfoot to the north-west.

From the Border Gate the Pennine Way keeps to the English side of the Border fence. This is a post and wire affair and seems inappropriate for an international frontier, but there is little or no stone for a wall. The ridge drops away sharply on the greener Scottish side and there are no foreground views; it is the sweep of peatland, of moss and heather, that stays in the memory. England can be a remarkably barren place. A recent plantation of spruce trees has rendered the slopes of the Usway Burn less hostile. Much of this area was once wooded, but Scottish raiders of the 14th and 15th centuries have been blamed for stealing, bit by bit, this Cheviot forest, with the result that by the 18th century nothing was left. The wilderness was a place for outlaws, including the Highlander Black Rory, who ran several illicit stills, including one at the foot of Davidson's Burn, which lies to the south-east of King's Seat.

The Way leads north-north-east past the triangulation point at King's Seat **A**, then turns north-east to follow the fence up towards Cairn Hill. Ahead is the great dome of The Cheviot, flanked by lesser hills bearing pimples of rocks or tors, fragments of andesite baked and hardened when the Cheviot granite welled up beneath an extinct volcano nearly 400 million years ago. The ascent towards Cairn Hill is steep and exacting. The little outcrop of rocks on the brow of the hill to the right is the Hanging Stone **113**, which separated the Middle March from the East March in the days when the Borderlands were governed by marcher lords. Underfoot the ground is sometimes treacherous and the vegetation is wind-blasted and sheep-cropped. There is bilberry, cowberry and crowberry, none of

Sheepfold

Sheepfold

Outer Byre Cleuch

Crooked Sike

Pennine Way

19

113 Hanging Stone

Crookedsike Head

Score Head

Cairn

570

550

Yearning Cleuch

Greengair Shin

Green Gair

540

Greengair Sike

Sheepfold

18

530

Kingsseat Shin

Cairn

520

Sheepfold

510

King's Seat

500

A 531

480

Murder Cleugh

450

Davidson's Burn

heepfold

Earthwork

Randy's Gap

17

490

Buttroadsike

Sheepfold

Hermoor Cleuch

480

Teviot Hills

Butt Roads

Pennine Way

524

Cairn

Sike

Outer Hare Cleugh

Sheepfold

FB

A

Lintlands

irn 542

16

550

Davidson's Linn

442

Ford

112

Waterfall

Ford

Clay Burn

Sheep

Sheepfold

430

88

89

Contours are given in metres
The vertical interval is 10m

147

which manage to produce very much fruit. There is also a lot of cloudberry, a dwarf relative of the raspberry.

The top of the hill is a quagmire and it is important to stick to the boardwalk, which leads to a junction of fences **B**. The Pennine Way heads left and is clearly signposted. Here you must decide whether to include a detour to take in The Cheviot **114**. At 2,674 feet (815 metres) it is a lofty summit, the highest in Northumberland, but because it is such a broad whaleback the views from the top are not especially good. However, the detour is not far and the path is now stone-flagged. Whatever you decide, the Way continues on its proper course at the stile heading north-west. It then crosses another quagmire of liquid peat via another boardwalk (this used to be one of the most dreadful sections of the whole route). To the right (north-east) is the headwater of the College Burn **115** which scores a course through a cleft in the side of the mountain and disappears from view. A little further on is Auchope Cairn **C**, which must be the most exposed and uncomfortable place on the whole ridge. The only birds likely to be seen here are snow buntings (which are quite regular, at almost any time of the year) and peregrines.

There is a small stone shelter which provides some protection from the wind, but it is a better idea to descend by the

Contours are given in metres
The vertical interval is 10m

Contours are given in metres
The vertical interval is 10m

Scotsman's Knowe, on the flanks of The Cheviot.

College Valley looking north-east, from Red Cribs towards Mounthooly.

north-west path and make for the more complete shelter **116** provided by a mountain refuge hut – similar to the one at Yearning Saddle on Lamb Hill and a vital sanctuary for anyone caught out by foul weather. From here the Way follows a clear path, still parallel with the Border fence, along a ridge linking 1,640-foot (500-metre) hills. The views are breathtaking, west across green pastures and the Bowmont Water to Windy Gyle, and east to the Hen Hole **117**, a hanging valley formed when the glaciers retreated 10,000 years ago. To the north is the College Valley, reputedly named after a coven of witches, beyond which is the coastal plain and the North Sea. The end of the Pennine Way lies only 7^1/$_2$ miles (12 km) away but this is still a dangerous place, unpredictable to the last. The wreckage of at least two lost aircraft lies on the sides of The Cheviot, and as recently as 1988 two walkers were killed in a snow avalanche on the Bizzle Crag beyond West Hill.

The Schil **118** is the last big hill on the route and one of the finest of all the Cheviot summits. The climb up to it is short and sharp, and the rocky crags on the top provide an exhilarating panoramic view. On the descent on the north side there are several tors (two in particular, **119**, frame the College Valley and help to make a good photograph). These tors are remnants of a metamorphic aureole, a circlet of hardened rocks, standing sentinel around The Cheviot.

The sweep downhill still follows the Border and leads to a ladder-stile **D** in the wall in a saddle or col between The Schil

Contours are given in metres
The vertical interval is 10m

151

and Black Hag. After this there is a ladder-stile **E** over the wall to the left; the path to the right leads down to Fleehope and Mounthooly, above the College Burn. It is possible to be picked up by car from either of these remote farms; although the 5-mile (8-km) road from Westnewton is private, the College Valley Estate allows a quota of permits for private vehicles. On the full Pennine walk such a deviation would be unthinkable, but pre-planned, an exploration of the valley would make an excellent weekend.

The Pennine Way now crosses the stile into Scotland; for several miles it will stay a stone's throw from the Border but you will not set foot in England again, so this is an important departure. A path leads north-west, below Corbie Craig and above the head of the Rowhope Burn, but after only a few hundred yards the Way forks **F**, offering the walker a choice between high- and low-level routes. You can either head right, back up to the ridge at Steerrig Knowe, or take the left fork over the col between Black Hag and The Curr to the west.

This latter, low-level, route, which soon resolves itself into a track, then follows a path north along the Halter Burn. It provides an easy and pleasant descent into Kirk Yetholm.

The other route, the high-level, keeps with the Border Ridge to the very end, to wring the last drop of excitement and endurance from the great walk. Certainly it follows a much more dramatic line, if you are still capable of it. From Steerrig Knowe **G** the Way heads north-north-east, keeping to the grassy ridge of Steer Rig, and losing height all the time. Ahead is the twin-cairned summit of Coldsmouth Hill.

To the west are Cheviot foothills and the green fields of the Bowmont. To the east is the bleached, treeless valley of the Trowup Burn **120**; sheep tracks contouring around Saughieside Hill emphasise the wide open spaces and the crazy way nature has of fitting tiny streams into great, ice-worn bowls. The stream itself resembles a pulled thread of wool, braiding or meandering sharply within the confines of its channel.

The terrain is grassy and firm. The last testing climb now lies ahead as the Way turns north-west to White Law **121**. Although of modest height, the slopes are steep, but the summit has a fine outlook, north-west over the Tweed Valley to the Lammermuir Hills and north-east to the Bowmont and the Till. Between these rivers lies Branxton where the Battle of Flodden, the conclusive defeat of the Scots, was fought in 1513. In the far distance is Berwick and the North Sea. To the east are the outer bastions of the Cheviots, above the mouth of the College near Hethpool.

Contours are given in metres
The vertical interval is 10m

153

These are Hare Law, Wester Tor, Easter Tor and Yeavering Bell. Yeavering, the most noteworthy of the group, is one of the most important archaeological sites in the Borders. Below it lies the site of the Anglo-Saxon palace of Ad Gefrin where the kings of Northumbria, Aethelfrith and Edwin, held court. The twin-peaked summit of the Bell itself, seen here in profile, is encircled by a stone rampart within which are the traces of 130 circular houses dating back to the Iron Age. (The Eildons, now to the west-north-west, have a similar large hill fort of the Votadini Tribe. These must have been important sites in pre-Roman times.)

Between White Law and Yeavering Bell lies Great Hetha, another Iron Age hill fort. Looking at a map suggests that most suitable hills had settlements of some kind; the population of these uplands was considerably greater 2,000 years ago than it is now. Wild goats, which still roam the slopes between Easter Tor and Yeavering, have seen civilisations wax and wane without making very much of an impression on the land.

The Way has nowhere left to go now and begins its final descent to the Bowmont Valley. Those who are walking just this section may feel a sense of satisfaction; those who have come

Contours are given in metres
The vertical interval is 10m

Journey's end after 268 miles is the bar of the Border Hotel in Kirk Yetholm.

Cross a ladder-stile **H** and head downhill, northwards, beside a wall until a track goes obliquely left **I**, signed at the wall. Here the Way leaves the Border and drops down along a green track. Ahead to the north-west is Green Humbleton **122**, a grassy hill crowned by another Iron Age hill fort, but the Way angles south-west around its lower slopes along ancient sheep tracks, then follows the Shielknowe Burn **J** down to meet the Halter Burn **K**.

The whole valley seems very bright and colourful after the hills, and the little Halter Burn, which draws most of its water from the western slopes of Steer Rig, is shallow and easily forded unless there has been very heavy rain on the ridge.

The Way meets a tarmac road at a cattle grid **L** and bears right to follow this west-north-west for the last mile of the journey. In the summer the lane is lined by green hawthorns and by walls dabbed white by lichen. There are banks of red campion and yellow broom and in the evening sunlight the ribbon of road shines gold against indigo shadows. At the end of this rainbow lies the little Border village of Kirk Yetholm **123**, famous now as the terminus of the Pennine Way. The 'finishing line' is generally held to be the sign at the bus stop or the bar of the Border Hotel. Your thoughts about the 256-mile (412-km) trail will depend on how you fared. Whatever the weather was like, no matter how treacherous the route and how tired you are, you will look back with a sense of achievement; you found time for something worthwhile and were up to the challenge. Some one at Edale may even now be looking to the north, wondering what lies ahead . . .

The Cheviot Hills

When Pennine Way veterans gather together, their most daunting stories tend to centre around the Cheviot bogs. This is not necessarily fair, but there is no doubt that the Cheviot traverse is a challenge, a high-level walk across the least populated hills in the country, often in poor weather and at the end of an exhausting two- or three-week trek. The best way to appreciate the finer points of the Cheviots is by spending a weekend in the area and approaching the Border Ridge from one of the radiating valleys (one of the routes out of Coquetdale is illustrated on page 141).

Glimpsed from afar the Cheviot Hills look like a jumble of frosted green domes. In fact they are grouped into a nebula of broad ridges with The Cheviot – a 2,674-foot (815-metre) whaleback of granite – at the heart of the constellation. The history of the Cheviots is quite different from that of the Pennines. They were created by the outpourings of a gigantic system of volcanoes 380 million years ago. The lava cooled to form andesite; at that time the spectacular range of mountains may well have resembled the modern Andes, from which the type of rock has earned its name. When the volcanoes fell silent an upwelling of magma beneath the hills left the Cheviots with a core of granite. Erosion gradually rounded the contours and stripped the covering of andesite from the top of the intrusion so that the highest ground now has several exposures of this harder rock at the surface. Because it cooled slowly deep under ground, granite is composed of large crystals (unlike extrusive volcanic rocks like the dolerite of the Whin Sill) which are made up of quartz, feldspar and mica. Where the hot granite touched the andesite it cooked or hardened it. Today, tors of this 'baked' andesite occur as an aureole around the high summits of The Cheviot and Hedgehope, visible on several of the hill crests and slopes to the east of the Pennine Way.

At one time the Cheviots were an island surrounded by a shallow sea, at another they were a headland looking out over an immense river depositing 1,000 feet (300 metres) of sand into a delta to the south and east. Eventually, rivers worked their way into faults in the massif, and valleys and hills were rounded by glaciers into the present rolling landscape. The andesite covers an area of 350 square miles (900 square km). Although rich in silica it is not so acidic as the granite or the Fell Sandstone to the south, so most of the foothills are covered in grass rather than heather and are called the White Land.

The route of the Pennine Way from Coquethead to Cairn Hill lies along a broad watershed of peat, but north of the treacherous Auchope mire (which is now crossed by a stone-flagged path) the ground improves and the stretch from The Schil to White Law is usually perfect. These two conical summits are as attractive and impressive as anything on the whole route, but of course most Pennine Way grafters will by this time have their minds fixed on home and their fund of stories.

Auchope Cairn may be the most inhospitable place along the whole Cheviot ridge for Pennine Way walkers; a consolation is the presence, at most times of year, of the delightful snow bunting – a rare sighting in most other parts of Britain.

The College Valley from Red Cribs. On the skyline to the left is the Schil, one of the last

...s along the Pennine Way before the descent to Kirk Yetholm.

159

USEFUL INFORMATION

Many of the characteristics that make the Pennine Way such an exciting prospect – the remote terrain, lack of roads and absence of towns – make it extremely difficult to plan a walk, because public transport and accommodation are limited. The following notes are intended as a précis of planning information, referring to more comprehensive sources of information where these are available. Details of transport and accommodation, which will be necessary for planning, are included for the whole of the Pennine Way, North and South. These are followed by details of useful regional addresses and a bibliography of titles of use on the northern half of the Way.

All Pennine Way walkers should be aware of the Pennine Way Association, which exists to protect the Way and to provide information and a forum in which organisations and individuals can get together to discuss matters relating to the Way: www.penninewayassociation.co.uk. For all enquiries email pennineway association@hotmail.com.

Transport

Local and national coach. Bus and rail information at Traveline.
Tel. 0871 2002233.
www.traveline.org.uk
www.traveldales.org.uk

Rail

National Rail Enquiries. Tel. 08457 484950. www.nationalrail.co.uk

Coach and Bus

National Express. Tel. 0121 6251122.
www.nationalexpress.co.uk

The principal public transport points along the Way, from south to north, are as follows:

Edale: some trains to and from Manchester and Sheffield stop at Edale.

Standedge: bus services between Huddersfield and Oldham extend to Manchester on Saturday.

Hebden Bridge: the Liverpool–Manchester–Leeds line passes through Hebden Bridge frequently during the week and also has a Sunday service.

Haworth: bus services are run by Keighley and District. Tel. 01535 603284; www.keighleyanddistrict. co.uk. The private steam-hauled Keighley and Worth Valley railway stops at Haworth, and takes you to the mainline station at Keighley. Tel. 01535 645214 for train times.

Thornton-in-Craven: a Pennine Motors coach (tel. 01756 795515) runs between Colne, Earby and Skipton, calling at Thornton-in-Craven. Trains from Colne and Skipton run to Leeds and Manchester.

Gargrave: Pennine Motors runs a service to Gargrave; from here there are buses to Skipton, Settle and Malham. Tel. 01756 795515.

Malham: Tel. 01756 795515 for buses to Skipton via Gargrave.

Horton in Ribblesdale: Settle and Carlisle trains run north to Carlisle and south to Leeds.

Hawes: a bus goes from here to Richmond. You can get a further bus to connect with BR at Darlington. For services from Hawes to

Garsdale, contact Hawes National Park Centre. Tel. 01969 666210.

Bowes: Central Coaches (also known as Voy) run a service to Barnard Castle. Tel. 01325 300604.

Thwaite and Keld: bus services run to Richmond Monday–Friday by Little Red Bus. Tel. 01423 526655, 0871 2002233, www.arrivabus.co.uk

Middleton in Teesdale has an infrequent bus service to Darlington. Tel. Arriva North East 0871 2002233 for the times.

Dufton: Robinson's Coaches run a bus service from Appleby (01768 351424), where there is a station on the Leeds–Settle–Carlisle line.

Alston: Wright Brothers runs bus and coach services from Alston to Haltwhistle via Slaggyford and to Hexham, Newcastle, Brampton and Carlisle. Tel. 01434 381200.

Twice Brewed: the Carlisle–Newcastle bus stops here hourly. Tel. 01228 819090 for details.

Hadrian's Wall: a bus service runs daily between Hexham and the main Wall sites during July and August. Tel. Northumberland National Park on 01434 605555.

Bellingham: Tyne Valley Coaches runs a service to Hexham for BR connection to Newcastle. Tel. 01434 602217.

Byrness: a National Express service runs daily from Newcastle to Edinburgh. Tel. 08717 818181. Munro's of Jedburgh run a daily bus between Jedburgh and Newcastle via Byrness. Tel. 01835 862253, www.munrosofjedburgh.co.uk

Kirk Yetholm: Munro's of Jedburgh run a daily service to Kelso, and another service from Kelso to Jedburgh, where connections can be made with Newcastle and Edinburgh.

Accommodation

The Pennine Way Association produces an invaluable Accommodation and Camping Guide with up-to-date lists of addresses. This can be viewed online at www.pennineway association.co.uk.

Members of the Ramblers' Association (address on page 163) will find some accommodation information in their yearbook. Otherwise, the best way to book overnight bed and breakfast is from the information on the Pennine Way website, www.nationaltrail.co.uk/ penninway, or through Tourist Information Centres or National Park centres. These will also have up-to-date lists of campsites. The Yorkshire Dales National Park also produces its own accommodation guide.

Tourist Information Centres (TICs) are also a useful source of local information. The following are the TICs in the vicinity of the Pennine Way:

Edale National Park Visitor Centre (a Peak National Park Centre), Fieldhead, Edale, Hope Valley, S33 7ZA. Tel. 01433 670207. email edale@peakdistrict.gov.uk

Hebden Bridge Canal and Visitor Centre, Butler's Wharf, New Road, Hebden Bridge, HX7 8AF Tel. 01422 843831. email hebdenbridge@ytbtic.co.uk

Haworth Visitor Information Centre, 2/4 West Lane, Haworth, West Yorkshire BD22 8EF. Tel. 01535 642329. Email haworthvic@bradford.gov.uk

Skipton TIC, 35 Coach Street, Skipton, North Yorkshire BD23 1LQ. Tel. 01756 792809. Email skipton@ytbtic.co.uk

Settle TIC, Town Hall, Cheapside, Settle, North Yorkshire BD24 9EJ. Tel. 01729 825192.
Email settle@ytbtic.uk

Horton in Ribblesdale Tourist Information Point, Pen-y-Ghent Café, Horton in Ribblesdale, North Yorkshire BD24 0HE. Tel. 01729 860333. email horton@ytbtic.co.uk

National Park Centre, Station Yard, Hawes, North Yorkshire DL8 3NT. Tel. 01969 666210.
Email hawes@ytbtic.co.uk

Middleton in Teesdale TIC, 10 Market Place, Middleton in Teesdale, County Durham DL12 0QG. Tel. 01833 641001. email middletonplus@compuserve.com

Appleby-in-Westmorland TIC, The Moot Hall, Boroughgate, Appleby-in-Westmorland, Cumbria CA16 6XE. Tel. 01768 351177. email tic@applebytowncouncil.fsnet.co.uk

Alston TIC, The Town Hall, Front Street, Alston, Cumbria CA9 3RF. Tel. 01434 382244.
email alston.tic@eden.gov.uk

Haltwhistle TIC, The Railway Station, Station Road, Haltwhistle, Northumbria NE49 9HN. Tel. 01434 322002. email haltwhistle@btconnect.com

Once Brewed Visitor Centre, Military Road, Bardon Mill, Hexham, Northumbria NE47 7AN. Tel. 01434 344396. email tic.oncebrewed@npa.org.uk

Hexham TIC, Wentworth Car Park, Hexham, Northumbria NE46 1QE. Tel. 01434 652220. email hexham.tic@tynedale.gov.uk

Kelso TIC, The Town House, The Square, Kelso, Borders TD5 7HF. Tel. 0870 608 0404.
bordersinfo@visitscotland.com

The principal overnight stopping places on the Way are, from south to north:

Edale: YH, B&B, camping

Crowden: YH, camping

Standedge: B&B, camping

Marsden: B&B

Mankinholes: YH

Ponden: B&B, camping

Earby: YH

Malham: YH, B&B, camping, bunkhouse barn

Horton-in-Ribblesdale: B&B, camping, bunkhouse

Hawes: YH, B&B, camping

Keld: B&B, camping, bunkhouse

Bowes: B&B, camping

Baldersdale: limited B&B, camping

Holwick: camping, bunkhouse barn

Langdon Beck: YH, B&B

Dufton: YH, B&B, camping

Garrigill: B&B, camping, bunkhouse barn

Alston: B&B, camping

Greenhead: B&B, camping

Once Brewed: YH, B&B, camping

Bellingham: B&B, camping

Byrness: YH, B&B

Coquetdale and Uswayford: limited B&B

Kirk Yetholm: YH, B&B

Useful addresses and websites

Borders Regional Council, Ranger Service. Tel. 01835 825060.

Durham Wildlife Trust, Rainton Meadow, Chilton Moor, Houghton-Le-Spring, DH4 6PU. Tel. 01915 843122. www.wildlifetrust.org.uk/durham

English Heritage, Customer Services, PO Box 569, Swindon, Wiltshire SN2 8YP. Tel. 0870 333 1181. www.english-heritage.org.uk

Forestry Commission: Kielder Forest District Office, Eals Burn, Bellingham, Hexham, Northumberland NE48 2HP. Tel. 01434 220242.

Long Distance Walkers' Association, www.ldwa.org.uk

National Trust, East Midlands Regional Office, Clumber Park Stableyard, Worksop, Nottinghamshire S80 3BE. Tel. 01909 486411.

National Trust (Northumbria Regional Office): Scots Gap, Morpeth, Northumberland NE61 4EG. Tel. 01670 774691.

Natural England (Headquarters), John Dower House, Crescent Place, Cheltenham, GL50 3RA. Tel.0845 600 3078, www.naturalengland.org.uk

Natural England, North-West Regional Office, 7th Floor, Bridgwater House, Whitworth Street, Manchester M1 6LT. Tel. 0161 237 1061.

Natural England, Leeds Office, Government Buildings, Otley Road, Lawnswood, Leeds LS16 5QT. Tel: 0113 230 3750.

Northumberland National Park: Eastburn, South Park, Hexham, Northumberland NE46 1BS. Tel. Hexham 01434 605555. www.nnpa.org.uk

Northumberland Wildlife Trust, The Garden House, St Nicholas Park, Jubilee Road, Newcastle upon Tyne NE3 3XT. Tel. 0191 284 6884. www.nwt.org.uk

Ordnance Survey, Romsey Road, Maybush, Southampton SO16 4GU. Tel. 0845 605 0505. www.ordnancesurvey.co.uk

Peak National Park Office, Aldern House, Baslow Road, Bakewell, Derbyshire DE45 1AE. Tel. 01629 816200. www.peakdistrict.gov.uk

Pennine Way Association, www.penninewayassociation.co.uk

Ramblers' Association, 2nd Floor, Camelford House, 87–90 Albert Embankment, London SE1 7TW. Tel. 020 7339 8500. www.ramblers.org.uk

Royal Society for the Protection of Birds (RSPB), The Lodge, Sandy, Bedfordshire SG19 2DL. Tel. 01767 680551, www.rspb.org.uk

Visit Britain, 1 Palace Street, London SW1E 5HE. Tel. 020 8846 9000. www.visitbritain.com

Welcome to Yorkshire, Dry Sand Foundry, Foundry Square, Holbeck, Leeds LS11 5WH. Tel. 0113 322 3500, www.yorkshire.com

Yorkshire Dales National Park, Colvend, Hebden Rd, Grassington, Skipton, North Yorkshire BD23 5LB. Tel. 01756 751600. www.yorkshiredales.org.uk.

Yorkshire Wildlife Trust, 1 St George's Place, York YO24 1GN. Tel. 01904 659570. www.ywt.org.uk

Youth Hostels Association, Trevelyan House, Dimple Road, Matlock, Derbyshire DE4 3YH. Tel. 0870 870 8808. www.yha.org.uk

Bibliography

Burton, Anthony, *Hadrian's Wall Path Official National Trail Guide* (Aurum, 2010).

Charlton, B., *Upper North Tynedale* (Northumbria Water Authority, 1987).

Collins M., *The Teesdale Way* (Cicerone, 1995).

Dobson, R. A. (ed.), *The Geology of North East England* (Natural History Society of Northumberland, 1980).

—, *Ordnance Survey Leisure Guide, Northumbria* (OS and AA, 1996).

Hadrian's Wall (Souvenir Guide) (English Heritage, 1987).

Hardy, G., *North to South along the Pennine Way* (Frederick Warne, 1983).

Hopkins, Tony, *Northumberland National Park Guide* (Pevensey, 2002).

Hopkins, Tony, *The Cheviot Hills* (Halsgrove, 2003).

Peel, J. H. B., *Along the Pennine Way* (David & Charles, 1972).

Pilton, B., *One Man and his Bog* (Corgi, 1986).

Wainwright, A., *Pennine Way Companion* (Frances Lincoln).

—, *Wainwright on the Pennine Way* (Frances Lincoln).

Wright, C. J., *A Guide to the Pennine Way* (Constable, 1987, 4th edn).

Wright G. N., *The Northumbrian Uplands* (David & Charles, 1989).

Northumberland National Park also produces a series of walks books covering circular routes in the Hadrian's Wall area, Coquetdale and the Cheviot Hills. For further details write to the address on page 163.

The Peak National Park, Yorkshire Dales National Park (addresses on page 163) and Calderdale Leisure Services Department of the Metropolitan Borough of Calderdale all produce good walks leaflets and other useful material. These may be obtained either by writing to the National Parks involved or by calling in at a visitor centre or tourist information centre. Information about Calderdale is best obtained from the Hebden Bridge Canal and Visitor Centre (see page 163).

Further information

For the latest information on the Pennine Way National Trail visit the official website: www.nationaltrail.co.uk/penninew ay. It provides all the information needed to prepare for the walk, from route map to accommodation guide. It also features stunning photography of the 268-mile (431-km) National Trail.

You can also order a useful pack of leaflets that provide details on the Trail, accommodation and public transport from:

The Pennine Way
National Trail Officer
Natural England
Yorkshire and Humberside
 Regional Office
25 Queen Street
Leeds LS1 2TW
Tel. 07900 608081

Ordnance Survey Maps covering the Pennine Way (North)

Landranger (1:50 000): 74, 75, 80, 91, 92

Explorer (1:25 000): OL16, Cheviot Hills; OL19, Howgill Fells& Upper Eden Valley; OL31, North Pennines, Teesdale & Weardale, OL42,Kielder Water & Forest; OL43, Hadrian's Wall

Motoring maps: Reach the Pennine Way (North) using the Road 3 and 4 Travel Maps

The Official Guides to all of

Cotswold Way
Anthony Burton

100 miles of quintessentially
English landscape

ISBN 978 1 84513 519 5

Cleveland Way
Ian Sampson

Over 100 miles of magnificent
walking on the North York Moors

ISBN 978 1 84513 520 1

Hadrian's Wall Path
Anthony Burton

Follow the Roman Wall
from coast to coast

ISBN 978 1 84513 567 6

**Peddars Way and
Norfolk Coast Path**
Bruce Robinson

90 miles from Breckland to
salt marsh and sea cliffs

ISBN 978 1 84513 570 6

North Downs Way
Neil Curtis and Jim Walker

Follow the chalk ridge across South-East
England all the way to the sea

ISBN 978 1 84513 602 4

South Downs Way
Paul Millmore

100 miles of glorious chalk downland
for the walker, cyclist and horse rider

ISBN 978 1 84513 565 2

Pennine Way
NORTH: Bowes to Kirk Yetholm
Tony Hopkins

140 miles of magnificent walking
through remote countryside

ISBN 978 1 84513 562 1

Offa's Dyke Path
SOUTH: Chepstow to Knighton
Ernie and Kathy Kay and Mark Richards

Follow the ancient earthwork up the Wye
Valley and alongside the Black Mountains

ISBN 978 1 84513 561 4

**Pembrokeshire
Coast Path**
Brian John

180 miles of clifftop, beach and cove
around the magnificent Welsh coast

ISBN 978 1 84513 563 8